PROUD OUTCASTS

# PROUD OUTCASTS

## THE GYPSIES OF SPAIN

By MERRILL F. MC LANE

*Photographs by the author*

**FRONTISPIECE**
*The piercing, questioning eyes and the body positions of these Gypsy children project the boldness, audacity and inquisitiveness of the Spanish Gypsy.*

CARDEROCK PRESS
*Cabin John, Maryland*

FRONT COVER
*The expressions of these Guadix cave dwellers reflect their inner strength and pride in being Gypsies.*

Copyright 1987 by Merrill F. McLane



**Library of Congress Cataloging-in-Publication Data**

McLane, Merrill F.
  Proud outcasts.

  Bibliography: p.
  Includes index.
  1. Gypsies—Spain—History. I. Title.
DX251.M35   1987          946'.00491497          86-70790
ISBN 0-938813-03-X (pbk.)

Printed in the United States of America



**CARDEROCK PRESS**
P.O. Box 56
Cabin John, MD 20818

# Preface

This book is a personal account of a voyage of discovery, not through space but into the hearts and souls of the *gitanos* or Gypsies of Spain, especially the two thousand five hundred considered to be the wildest and yet most traditional of Spanish Gypsies who live in Guadix within the province of Granada. I took part in their daily lives over a period of ten years and so I have written about them as friends, not as literary characters or shadow figures of a social class or race.

These are not fictional Gypsies, the story-book distortions. Nor are they the professional flamenco artists of Seville and Granada. They are Gypsies who long ago stopped roaming, but who held onto some of the occupations of their nomadic ancestors while acquiring ones more suitable to a settled life. They are horse traders, smithies, lottery vendors, bootblacks and harvesters of olives and tomatoes. Their day-to-day pleasures are sipping wine in their cave taverns while chatting and playing cards and dominoes with their Gypsy and non-Gypsy friends. But these same Gypsies have passions that run near the surface; if their honor is challenged, they will pull their knives, prepared to fight to the death.

Their home is Andalusia, the Spanish South and the Gypsy heartland. Even in Andalusia, life has not been easy for them. From the reign of Ferdinand and Isabella in the late 1400s until Carlos III in the late 1700s, Gypsies everywhere were ordered to settle down, to stop using their language, and to mingle with the other inhabitants. Despite these pressures to conform, they continued to remain a race apart.

Gypsies have fascinated Western man ever since they penetrated Europe in the 1400s after their four-hundred year trek from their ancestral home in India. In Spain, they were established literary characters by the 1500s, well before Cervantes used them in *The Little Gypsy Girl* and *The Dogs' Colloquy*. Two centuries later, the remarkable George Borrow described his adventures with them in *The Bible in Spain* and in *The Zincali*. Voltaire, Wordsworth, Sir Walter Scott and

Ralph Waldo Emerson wrote about them; and in 1888 in Edinburgh, the Gypsy Lore Society was founded to exchange information on Gypsies. In this century Walter Starkie, a scholar of Spanish literature at Dublin University, described his experiences with the Spanish Gypsies in *In Sara's Tents*. Irving Brown from Columbia University wrote about flamenco and its performers in *Deep Song* as did Bertha Quintana and Lois Floyd in *Qué Gitano!*

I first became interested in Gypsies as a boy in Massachusetts when my mother cautioned me to avoid them should they come to our town in their horse-drawn caravans selling baskets of woven sweet grass. She feared that they would steal our chickens, or even worse, kidnap me. To my disappointment, I never saw any Gypsies in those days because they were no longer visiting our part of the state. Nonetheless, stimulated by my mother's stories, I would sometimes lie awake in my room at night hoping for the return of these mysterious people who had so frightened her.

My curiosity about the Gypsies continued during my university years and work life, and when I was casting about for a project to challenge me after retiring, it came to me: *I would go to Spain, meet the Gypsies and write about them.* I had never been to Spain, but it, too, fascinated me.

Even as I committed myself to the project, I wondered about the abyss that separated the culture of the Gypsies from mine. I might be unable to communicate with them. What would my response to these strange people reveal about myself? Was John Sampson correct when he wrote in *The Wind on the Heath* that a person's reaction to the Gypsies was a touchstone to his personality? If James Michener in *Iberia* conceded that he had not succeeded in unraveling the peculiarities of Spain, would I be able to unravel the peculiarities of the Gypsies?

Despite these doubts, the notion grew on me, and I went ahead with preparations before retiring, brushing up on my Spanish, reading all that I could find in the Library of Congress on Gypsies, and taking university courses in cultural anthropology. I also studied linguistics to help with the Indic-related Romany language of the Gypsies, known in Spain as Caló. Spanish-Caló dictionaries had appeared every generation or so for the past one hundred and fifty years, but except for George Borrow's work of the 1830s, most were armchair collections, unrelated to the spoken word. Did Gypsies in Spain still *speak* Caló?

During my reading, I became aware that the Gypsies were hiding much about themselves from the non-Gypsy population. How, for example, did they hold onto their Gypsiness under the pressure of a dominant culture? What part did Caló play in their Gypsiness? There were so many unknowns I decided I would keep my voyage an open-ended quest. If I penetrated Gypsy life, the Gypsies would tell me what they considered to be important about themselves.

My wife and I made two exploratory trips to Spain in the early 1970s. Other journeys would follow. I used the approach favored by Havelock Ellis, who recommended in *The Soul of Spain* that a country with such a strong character should be mediated over between a succession of visits.

We kept an eye out for Gypsies, talking with them whenever we could. We gave pesetas to Gypsy mothers begging with their children in the subways of Madrid and in the cafés of Torremolinos in response to their pleas of *"para la niña"* (for the baby) and in Córdoba we rode in a *coche-caballo*, the horse-drawn carriage driven by one of the Gypsies who have a near monopoly on the trade; we browsed through Gypsy antique shops in Ubeda and Marbella, talked with Gypsy hotel workers in Mallorca, bantered with Gypsies selling watches and lace in the lovely park along Málaga's waterfront, and on the island of Madeira, learned from Portuguese Gypsies that their Romany is about the same as Caló. During these voyages we saw only a wagon or two of nomadic Gypsies, because most of Spain's 150-200,000 Gypsies are settled.

Within Andalusia we focused on the province of Granada with its many Gypsies. In the city of Granada, a Spanish acquaintance took us to a bar among the flamenco caves at Sacromonte, introducing us to two male Gypsy dancers. One of them, tall and handsome, had—we were told—killed three men. Was it the truth? Or was it a tale the non-Gypsies told to show how savage and different the Gypsies are?

We ruled out Granada and Sacromonte as places to study the Gypsies in more detail. The floods of 1963 had forced the Gypsies to abandon their homes on Sacromonte except for the flamenco caves at the foot of the hill, and I was not interested in flamenco performers. Spanish friends had told us that the most primitive of the Spanish Gypsies lived in Guadix, a city of fourteen thousand, thirty-five miles to the east of Granada, so we went there, and saw Gypsies walking along the streets as though they were at home. Guadix looked promising.

On our visit to the city the following year, however, we both felt that life in that provincial city would be too difficult for my wife, so she returned home. On the long drive back through the mountains to Guadix from the airport in Granada, I realized that I would be lonely without her.

Ahead was an unknown reception in a city of Spanish speakers where I knew no one. There was no certainty that I would meet Gypsies, let alone have them accept me. Later, I realized that in addition to loneliness, I was also experiencing a kind of cultural shock from the mere anticipation of the plunge into a totally Spanish world. (On future trips I found the best technique for entering this world was to jump into it alone at the port of entry, severing relations as soon as possible with fellow Americans and other foreigners.)

I was driving through a pine-covered pass. High against the skyline to my right were the outlines of rough walls and towers of natural stone. Puzzled, I stopped the car and began the long ascent on foot for a closer look. They turned out to be the remains of a military outpost. (I later found out that they were used during the Spanish Civil War.) By then, I was feeling better. The exertion of climbing in the dry air to an elevation of four thousand feet had been good for me. It had given me a respite before descending into Guadix, and although I had not entirely shaken off my anxiety, my courage was returning. From then on, I moved with more confidence toward my goal of discovering the secrets of the Spanish Gypsies.

# Contents

# 1

# A Gypsy On Stage

Her skin was of Egyptian brown:
Haughty, as if her eye had seen
Its own light to a distance thrown...
*William Wordsworth*

As I looked up the hill toward the cave city, I saw a tall woman coming down the street, walking purposefully. She had a free-flowing stride and swung her arms vigorously, yet gracefully. She had to be a *gitana* (Gypsy woman), because only Gypsies walked that way. When she got closer, I saw that it was Isabel, but a different Isabel from the mild-mannered wife of Antonio, the bootblack, whom I knew in their cave. She was projecting an attitude which said to the city dwellers, "Look at me! I am a Gypsy woman! If you don't like it, that's too bad!"

This was a proud *gitana* who, with her splendid gait, might still be walking through Afghanistan en route to the West from India a thousand years ago rather than descending from the cave city of Guadix to the market place. She could have been the *gitana*, described by Spain's nobel prize-winning poet, Ramón Jiménez in *Platero and I*:

There she comes down the street, holding her body straight and erect...without so much as a glance at anyone.

On entering the city of houses from the cave city, Isabel had become an actress—her stage the city streets, and her audience the shopkeepers and their wives. For her performance that morning, she had abandoned her nondescript cave attire and was wearing a bright yellow sweater and a knee-length red skirt. These vivid colors made her stand out from the non-Gypsy women, most of whom dressed in black, a color *gitanas* seldom used.

Pepe Falcó's wife, who operated a paper store with him, had said, "You know, the Gypsies have a monopoly on the use of bright colors. Even if I wanted a red skirt, I would not buy one. My friends would say that I was wearing clothing typical of a Gypsy."

Except for color, though, Isabel dressed the same as other city women. She kept up with womens' fashions by watching television and by looking in shop windows. She didn't wear mini-skirts, but neither did the non-Gypsies in Andalusia. She also avoided slacks and blue jeans, although Gypsy teenagers wore them. (A few old *gitanas* wore ankle-length dresses of a by-gone era, but so did some of the old non-Gypsy women.) Showing her independence, Isabel did not wear an apron as did most married Gypsies when in the city of houses.

I had been observing Isabel from my post on the balcony of my room after breakfast. It was about ten o'clock that summer morning three months after my arrival in Guadix. The sky, a deep Andalusian blue, was filled with swallows darting after flies. The shops along the street were open for business and the girls who worked in them had finished their daily mopping of the sidewalks in front. One of the shop owners across from the hotel had just redecorated the window of his *camisería* (shirt store), with several T-shirts imprinted with the names of American universities. The street was teeming with shoppers, some already returning from the market with filled shopping bags; others like Isabel just arriving.

Before Isabel reached my hotel, two other *gitanas* joined her. Continuing down the street, they did not keep in step like non-Gypsy women. They avoided an even formation, constantly changing positions like a flock of birds.

A few minutes after they had passed from my sight, I left my room and walked toward the indoor market. They were chatting together on the sidewalk. Two had already been inside the market and were holding melons and large sacks of potatoes, for *gitanas* not only do the family shopping but the carrying as well. I had seen one of them a few days before struggling up the hill under the weight of a bed frame.

I stopped in front of a shop across from them, and used the window as a mirror to observe the splashes of color coming from their red, orange, yellow, green and blue blouses, sweaters and skirts. I had noticed from seeing Isabel close-up in her cave that she was a careless dresser. It was the same with the others—snaps on skirts were askew and buttons on blouses were missing or not buttoned. One *gitana* reached inside her blouse to adjust her brassiere. Another had a partially bare midriff. *Payo* (non-Gypsy) men passing by took note of it, but said nothing for their own safety, saving their remarks until out of earshot.

The *gitanas'* hair-dos were typical of the Gypsies of Andalusia, the hair drawn straight back, caught up with a ribbon or small clasp in back of the head, and then falling in a pony tail to their shoulders. One of them, though, had spit curls on her forehead like a flamenco dancer and had parted her hair on the side. They were all wearing earrings, pendant and hooped, gold and silver; one was centered with a red stone; another was made of pearls. Each of them had a ring or two on both hands. One was wearing a necklace of orange beads, another a bracelet. Their jewelry was more conspicuous than that of the non-Gypsy women, but it lacked the gaudiness of the heavy silver or gold bracelets Gypsies in other parts of the world wore.

The son of a shop-keeper, a university student in Granada, stopped to talk with me. When I told him that I was looking at the *gitanas*, he asked, pointing to Isabel, "Do you notice how that one is standing? It is a typical Gypsy stance. See how her hands are on her hips with her thumbs on the front of the hip bone and her fingers on the upper part of her buttocks. And look how she accentuates her position by thrusting out her belly."

"What about that *gitana* carrying a baby on her hip as though he were a sack of vegetables?" I asked.

"That's a Gypsy trait," he said. "Never does a Castilian [the local word for non-Gypsy] do that. If she did, someone would remind her that she is holding her baby 'like a Gypsy.' And look," he added, "none of them has an umbrella, although it rained earlier this morning."

"I've noticed that. Also, I've never seen Isabel or the others with purses or baby carriages."

Suddenly a loud exchange between Isabel and another *gitana* began. Onlookers slowed to listen, and the audience of store owners moved to their store fronts.

Isabel, while eating a piece of bread, said to the other, *"Anda Ya! Qué te gusta beber mente para que se te ponga gorda la pepitilla!"* (Hey! How you like to drink mint to fatten your clitoris!)

The other replied, "And you! Woman who makes love in the doorway!"

Isabel, her adversary, and the others laughed and continued up the hill toward their cave homes, starting to exit from the city stage after having once more provided their audience with a scene to be relived for days in the city bars and homes.

"Tell me," I said to my friend, "Why did Isabel say that about mint?"

"Many Andalusians, not just Gypsies, believe that drinking mint tea increases the sexual potency of both men and women."

Although I had assumed the *gitanas* had finished their role playing, I was mistaken. Just beyond the church of Santiago, a quarrel broke out among them. The shouting was so loud that it bounced off the walls of the buildings fronting the narrow street. The noise was too much for the apartment dwellers who lived above the street and who ordinarily welcomed these disputes. Windows opened, and voices called down, "Quiet! Quiet!"

Isabel and the others shouted right back at them in a mixture of Spanish and Caló, *"Achanta la mui! Achanta la mui!"* (Shut your mouth! Shut your mouth!)

Isabel's angry eruption was one of the many emotions she could project with the skill of an actress. Meek one moment, she could become menacing the next; madonna-like in her cave home, she could assume a savage appearance to strangers who entered the cave area. A relaxed, warm neighbor and mother, she could be a haughty performer on the Guadix stage.

The shop-keepers, aware of the various faces of the *gitanas*, took this into account when dealing with them. "I fear scenes in my store," Falcó said. "Under one pretext or another, they return their purchases and claim a refund. I don't encourage their business."

Despite Isabel's spontaneity, she was bound by unwritten rules of conduct that applied to all *gitanas*. "They can't smoke tobacco, you know," Antonio had told me, and I never saw Isabel or other *gitanas* smoke. (Gypsy boys, though, begin to smoke at the age of ten or eleven.) "She must also be careful," Antonio said, "about talking to men in the city." When she passed me in the street, the only greeting Isabel gave was a look of recognition—and, for my part, I usually gave only a slight nod. To do more, would start Castilian tongues wagging, or worse, would cause a dangerous reaction among Gypsies. As it developed, even these slight recognition signals were later to contribute to a perilous episode.

Isabel could drink wine and beer, but as Antonio put it in Caló, "Tapiya poco." (She drinks only a little.) If Antonio went into a bar, Isabel waited for him on the sidewalk or just inside the door. He would usually drink up quickly and not keep her waiting. In a few bars, such as Joaquin's across from the Santiago church, she sometimes had a

*Isabel with her husband, Antonio the bootblack, and one of her children in the City of Caves.*

small glass of beer with Antonio, which she drank quickly and then left with him. Another restriction, one that Isabel did not always observe, was that the *romí* (Gypsy for wife), when walking alongside her husband, remains about a half pace behind him.

If her husband provokes his wife, though, she may make her own rules. That morning after Isabel and the others had left, a middle-aged *gitana*, playing her part on the Guadix stage, came up the street berating her spouse, to the enjoyment of the shop-keepers and their clients. She was striding vigorously, her long, dark pony tail jerking from one shoulder to the other as she poured out a tirade. At the same time, she was banging a big stick on the asphalt which she threatened to use. He, the poor fellow, was slinking up the sidewalk in front of her trying to appear as inconspicuous as possible. Perhaps he had spent too much money on wine or had looked at another *gitana*. Whatever it may have been, he was regretting it. Before they were out of earshot, I heard fragments of her shouts. "What a man God has given me! *Qué hombre!*"

As I puzzled over the meaning of Isabel's aggressiveness along the city streets, I realized again that I had to develop my own explanation for why Gypsies acted differently from non-Gypsies. My reading didn't help. Others who had described the unusual behavior of Gypsy women had not taken the next step of asking "why?" They probably would have been satisfied with Falcó's view, "It is because they are Gypsies. They are different."

I admired the way Isabel carried herself. Aware that the store owners detested Gypsies, it took courage to show off her pride in being a Gypsy. But this did not explain why she purposefully antagonized them.

Was there a pattern in the public conduct of the Gypsy woman? There seemed to be. Wordsworth's haughty Gypsy with "skin of Egyptian brown," and Ramón Jiménez' Gypsy, "straight and erect" looking at no one were acting to impress their uniqueness on *payo* observers and so was Isabel. Flaunting her Gypsiness was to remind the merchants and their wives that the Gypsies were still a race apart despite their residence of over five hundred years in Spain, and that they intended to remain that way.

# 2

# City Life and Friends

The one-star Hotel Comercio where I stayed was my sanctuary in Guadix, providing me with privacy to write and think. Jesús, the proprietor, gave me a comfortable room with bath. La Señora, his mother, and María, the plump cook who lived in a cave at the top of the steep street running up from the hotel, prepared delicious meals.

Miguel, the lone waiter, served them. His duties included cleaning the dining room, which he kept spotless. A sandy-haired Castilian, born and raised in a cave, he was ever solicitous of my needs. After serving my breakfast of thick slices of bread—toasted on top of a black stove—with butter, jam and pitchers of hot milk and coffee, he would sit down at my table, and we would discuss a wide range of subjects from local nicknames to *curanderos* (folk healers). We talked as friends, and our chats were a pleasant preparation for my day in the city or the countryside.

The balcony of my room, from where I had observed Isabel's entry into the city, was my lookout. During my first weeks in the city, I spent at least an hour each day using it, as Washington Irving had used his balcony in the Hall of Ambassadors during his residence in the Alhambra above Granada in 1829, to view what Irving called the "busy scene of human life." Besides Gypsies and other cave dwellers passing below me, there were milkmen with their cans on the backs of motorcycles, a Guardia Civil walking briskly past with a pistol dangling at his hip, mules pulling a wagon of sand, a woman leading a burro,

*From one of these balconies in the Hotel Comercio author McLane observed the pageant of city life passing along the narrow street below.*

delivery boys riding on their bicycles, a tall priest in his black, ankle-length cassock striding along the sidewalk.

Late one evening I had just fallen asleep when I was awakened by the wail of a voice singing flamenco. Its scales and intervals, so different from those of western music, startled me. Leaping from my bed, I dashed to the balcony in time to see a solitary Gypsy youth strolling up the street returning to his cave-home, singing for his own pleasure:

One pain leaves, another comes
One sorrow, another sorrow.

Like most Spanish hotels, there was no protection from the noise in the street below. Eventually, I acquired the knack of shutting out the sound of motorcycles, the shrieking of overburdened, small trucks,

*The Comercio crew: Miguel the waiter in the striped shirt who became the author's friend; the laundry woman who believed in evil eye; Maria the cook; the chamber-maid, Maria's daughter and a friend.*

and the loud voices of the city residents, who rarely quieted down until after midnight. I then slept easily, tuning in to the pleasant sounds of church clocks ringing out the hours and, in the morning, to the tinkling of the bells around the neck of the old, grey mule who patiently pulled the city trash wagon.

The hotel, of course, had disadvantages. Like most hotels in Europe, the windows had no screens. This gave the flies access to the room — there were no mosquitoes. At first they bothered me, but since they limited their activity to flying in circles near the ceiling by day, and disappeared at night I learned to ignore them.

Though I was impatient to meet Gypsies and to visit them in their cave-homes, getting acquainted was not easy. For several weeks I was bound to the city streets, unable to penetrate the city of caves where half the city's population lived, including five hundred Gypsies. I had been moving cautiously, because I had been warned about the dangers of dealing with Gypsies. A graduate student at the University of Granada, who had been observing Gypsies in that city, had shown me his snap-blade knife. "I always carry it when among them," he said.

Also, I had not forgotten an unpleasant experience near Zarauz on the north Atlantic coast when I boldly walked up to a Gypsy family to take photographs and was stoned for my disregard of good manners. It was embarrassing, too, because it took place in front of my wife who, fearing for my safety, drove our rented automobile quickly to my side to rescue me.

I curbed my impatience. I realized that I should learn something about the city and the attitudes of its non-Gypsy residents toward the Gypsies so that I could better understand Gypsies when I did meet them. I called on the mayor, school teachers, priests and the town clerks of villages, telling them that I was interested in the traditions of the region and in its people. I found out from interviews there were about 2500 Gypsies in the region—the government maintains no separate data on them.

The city was dirty and noisy, just as Gerald Brennan had described it in *South from Granada* based on his visits in the 1920s. I found, however, the warmth and openness of the residents to the stranger compensated for the unattractiveness of the city. A proud people, they called themselves *Guadijeños*, or *Accitanos* after the Roman colony Acci, one of the predecessors of the present-day city.

Of all the *Accitanos*, Pepe Falcó, who had a stationery store across from the Bar Dólar, was the most helpful, and we became friends.

Classically Spanish with a long, ivory-tinted face, set off by a short, black mustache, he had the mannerisms of a grandee. He loved Guadix. "Guadix is my home town," he said. "I missed it during my years working away."

I visited his shop daily where he and his wife introduced me to the clients they believed would interest me: a priest from an outlying village who had served in Venezuela, a visiting school director from Barcelona, and other store owners, thus giving me a better perspective on the city and its Gypsies than if I had been only with Gypsies.

One day, Falcó said to me, "Their psychology is different than ours. I am confused by them. They are lazy and untrustworthy, but they have qualities I admire."

"What are these qualities?" I asked.

"The wives honor their husbands. Prostitution is rare among them. The men, though, are like us. They have an eye for other women."

A poet from Barcelona raised in the caves of Guadix, who had just entered the store, on overhearing our conversation said, "The women have long respected their husbands. In the 1600s Cervantes wrote about it in the *Dogs' Colloquy*. Doesn't that make the Gypsies more Spanish than we are? Some of us no longer treasure the family as the Gypsies do."

"I don't know," replied Falcó. "Something else is different about them. They can do with so few material comforts."

"Like clothing or food?" I asked.

"Yes. I remember one cold winter evening when I was a young man drinking in a bar. A Gypsy burst through the door wearing tattered sandals and no coat. Standing erect, as though impervious to the cold, he asked, 'What would you like me to sing for you?' He wasn't requesting money, and would not have accepted it if offered. He was showing his ability to rise above physical discomfort."

A priest, who was buying a book, echoed Falcó's sentiments, "I just don't understand them. They are a peculiar race. They never change. They go their own way."

"The Gypsies," the poet said, "are a race that suffers the consequences of its liberty. They are the outcasts of Iberia."

Falcó and the priest were not the only ones perplexed. Sometimes when I was observing Gypsies near the Plaza de Abastos, out of the corner of my eye I would see Castilians staring at them just as intently—still trying to understand these unassimilated people, five hundred and fifty years after their entry into Spain.

Some of the poor non-Gypsies made similar remarks about the Gypsies that the store owners did, but I was to find out later that the Castilian cave dwellers among whom they lived did not. They looked on them first as neighbors, and then as Gypsies.

When listening to the criticisms of Falcó and his friends, I heard no mention of cannibalism, which the Gypsies have supposedly practiced through the centuries. No one had heard of the Guadix shepherd who, according to an early Spanish writer, was welcomed by a band of Gypsies high in the Sierra Nevada only to find that they planned to eat him.

Falcó, however — as had my mother — knew about their reputation for kidnapping. "Before the 1936-1939 Civil War," he said, "nomadic Gypsies, known as *Zíngaros*, used to visit the city in horse-drawn caravans. The women wore long, colorful skirts, and the men played the violin and repaired copper pots, skills unknown to Spanish Gypsies. On one of their visits, a Castilian girl ran away to join a Gypsy youth. Her brothers, armed with clubs, ran to the campsite to retrieve her. They were too late. The Gypsies had left. Later, the parents claimed she had been kidnapped."

I was amused to learn from the Falcós that hotel keepers in Mallorca seek Gypsies out as waiters, because to the North European guests they appear to be more Spanish — i.e. darker — than the Castilians. They also told me that Gypsies have been cast as American Indians by motion picture companies which film westerns south of Guadix.

Reminiscent of myths in the United States about Negroes, male Gypsies are reputed to have larger genitals than non-Gypsies. An official in Guadix showed me a citation a Castilian woman brought against a Gypsy, *un tal pijorro*, one with a large penis. She claimed he had molested her. "Perhaps he was only trying to live up to his reputation," the official said.

I looked in vain in Guadix for Gypsy fortune-telling parlors. "How odd!" I thought. "Here I am in the heart of Gypsy country, and I haven't seen any signs of card-reading or palmistry." On my next visit to Falcó's shop, I asked him and a pharmacist from next door if Gypsy women told fortunes.

"Not any more. Thirty or forty years ago they told fortunes to Castilian women, even to my mother, but they never had the store front operations the way they did in Montreal where I once worked," said Falcó.

"There is a *gitana* in Málaga today who is well known," said the pharmacist, who also owned a pharmacy in Málaga. "Foreign tourists from all over the Costa del Sol come to visit her."

In a later visit to Falcó's shop, when I told him that I planned to go among the Gypsies to study their way of life, Falcó and his friends were quick to discourage me.

"The Gypsies," one said, "are dirty, lazy and deceitful. *"Qué lástima del agua que se beben*!" (A pity on the water they drink!)

"They want to eat without working," said another.

"How do they make a living?" I asked. "They can't all be shoe-shiners and lottery vendors."

"A lot of them are," a merchant said. "Some sell cloth and clothing — even shoes. A few weave baskets. But no antique dealers as in Seville."

"Who would buy from them?" Falcó asked.

"I've heard," I said, "that in Switzerland and Germany they work on construction."

"Some do that here."

"But we don't let them collect junk the way they do in Madrid," said a city official who had just come into the shop. "And remember," he added, "the real Spanish do not trust them."

They would have agreed with Somerset Maugham who, after visiting Andalusia, referred to the Gypsies as a "bastard race." The only businessman I heard defend the Gypsies was a beer distributor. "You know," he said in Falcó's store, "for the Gypsies to be acceptable to us, they must conform to our ways."

"But why can't they be like us?" Falcó asked.

The poet, on vacation from Barcelona, joined the conversation. "If they conform, they are no longer Gypsies."

"That's just it," said the beer distributor. "They are in a dilemma. To be Gypsies, they can't be like us."

"Don't some Gypsies do the same work as Castilians?" I asked.

"Yes, but they remain different inside," he said.

"García Lorca called the Gypsies the most aristocratic element in Spain, the keepers of Andalusian truth," said the poet. "If they conform, all this would be lost. If they hadn't held onto old Spanish rhythms, we would have no flamenco today."

"That wouldn't bother me," said Falcó. "I don't like flamenco."

Falcó was not alone among the Guadix merchants in disliking flamenco. They would never follow the example of Morón de la Frontera near Seville where a bust of the Gypsy guitarist, Diego del Gastor, has been erected in the city park.

"Do you remember," the poet continued, "what a poet —I believe it was Salvador Rueda —said about the Gypsies? Something about their being spat on and stoned during their travels about the world."

"Why shouldn't they be? What else would you expect?" asked Falcó.

The poet took another approach. "They love their independence the way we do. Also their freedom."

Falcó shook his head in disagreement.

The Falcós not only discouraged me from seeing Gypsies because of their undesirability, but concerned over my safety, said, "Look out for their knives! When a Castilian smiles he means it, but when a Gypsy smiles, his knife is at your belly." To illustrate the blood thirstiness of the Gypsies, they told me that a few years ago two Gypsies were fighting with knives near the park with their wives present. One Gypsy slashed the other so badly that his intestines protruded. When he stepped away from his opponent, his wife pushed the organs back into place, and urged him, "to get back and fight."

I found that this fear of the Gypsies extended into the armed forces, even though Gypsies must serve in them. A sergeant in the Spanish Air Force, to whom I gave a lift on the road to Alicante, was surprised that I planned to go among the Gypsies alone, and reluctantly accompanied me to a Gypsy quarter in Murcia.

Falcó had also told me that I should visit the open-air market, held on Saturdays and known as the *Sábado*, if I wanted to see the real Guadix. I followed his advice and so enjoyed it that I went every Saturday. Live chickens, goats, hogs, and rabbits tied by their hind legs were for sale; and fruits and vegetables; rugs, pots, pans, earthenware, chinaware, framed prints; shoes; clothing and cloth.

I walked past the portable stalls, watching the vendors as they hawked their goods. City officials and their wives strolled through the market along with working-class Castilians from the cave complex. A member of the city council, knowing that I had an interest in Gypsies, walked up to a middle-aged, sturdily built *gitana*, who was selling fragments of cloth, introducing me as an *extranjero* (foreigner) who wanted to talk to her. Without hesitation, she announced in a rich, full voice, "*Soy de la raza gitana*". (I am of the Gypsy race.) She wanted it understood before we talked that I knew she was a Gypsy.

I saved the visit to the horse-trading area for the last, because I enjoyed it so much. It was off by itself at one end of the market, beyond the stands of melons and trucks of goats, pigs, and sheep along the

*The Gypsy horse dealer, one-eyed Sebastian, astride his white mule with other traders at the Saturday market.*

bank of the River Guadix, the Wadi Ash of the Moors. There were more flies there than in the rest of the market, because of the animal droppings and a pile of offal from the slaughter house, moved later to another location. I watched in disbelief while a four-year-old Gypsy boy waded through the mess up to his knees, sorting out the edible fragments with a stick.

One Saturday as I stood looking at the animals, perhaps fifty in all, mostly burros, the remainder horses and mules, and at the traders, Gypsy and non-Gypsy, known locally as *marchantes*, an old man with an unshaven face, standing nearby, said to me, "Not many animals for sale these days. Too many tractors and automobiles."

Wearing a sweat-stained felt hat and a worn, woolen jacket, he looked as though he had slept in his clothes. He also had on a vest, buttoned in spite of the hot sun, and as soiled as his coat. He was leaning on a staff with a short piece of rope attached to it. These were the marks of a trader, so I said to him, "Are you a *marchante?*"

"I used to be," he replied.

"But not a Gypsy."

He smiled, showing his black teeth. "No, I'm a *payo*," he said, pronouncing the "y" something like an English "j."

Just then a one-eyed Gypsy, riding a white mule, stopped to talk. Sebastian, as my new acquaintance called him, looked like a pirate. He had a prominently displayed gold tooth and was wearing a purple *faja* (sash) around his waist.

"Any sales?" Sebastian asked.

"Few," replied the old man.

Sebastian left, and the old man, pointing to a group of men talking loudly, said, "It always goes the same way. The buyer and seller start with the asking price. Then they separate to discuss it with friends and in-between men. They get together again, only to separate after a few minutes. In the meantime, the owner shows off his animal. This can continue all morning without a sale.  Talk, talk, talk."

A tall Gypsy came by leading several well-groomed, strong-looking horses. "That's Luis de los Caballos," the old man said. "He's from Benalúa, a near-by village. He and other Gypsies from Benalúa are here every Saturday. Gypsies from another village, Alcudia, four miles to the south, also make the trip into Guadix. There's one there."

I looked, and saw a well-dressed, chocolate-complexioned Gypsy with a black mustache who looked like a Hollywood movie star of the 1920s. "He's rich," the old man said. "He doesn't come by horse along the dry river beds. He comes in a van."

My new friend walked over to look at some horses, and then returned, saying, "These people don't come just to buy and sell. They come to see each other, to talk about horses. There are too many horse traders to make a living. During the week they take odd jobs."

He was correct about the social life at the *Sábado*, particularly among the Gypsies. They didn't come alone. They made it a family affair. Wives and children were arriving, some on the backs of burros and some walking behind their *rom*, husbands in Caló, mounted on their horses. I never saw a Gypsy girl or woman on a horse. Horses were reserved for males, and were for pleasure, not for work. The younger Gypsy children were playing among the animals. The older boys were showing them off to potential buyers, and the women watched the proceedings. About one o'clock, the family would sit under the shade of one of the few trees on the litter-strewn ground and eat some bread, fruit and sausage.

In those days, I had no idea that someday I would know these aristocratic-looking Gypsies by their nicknames. Getting to know them, though, was a slow process. Three or four years passed before I was drinking with them in their village bars and talking to them in Caló.

A trader kicked at a dog, reminding me that in Guadix, both Gypsies and non-Gypsies were not fond of animals. Dogs and cats were skin and bones. There were exceptions, however. The Falcós had a mongrel dog of whom they were fond, and I have seen Gypsies and non-Gypsies

*Gypsy boys at the outdoor market proudly showing off their burro who is bedecked with a tasseled bridle and a colorful blanket.*

riding their burros along country roads in the hot summer sun with their tired dogs perched on the backs of their animals. Then, too, the ornate, hand-made harnesses on some of the animals must, I felt, reveal affection toward them. It was unlikely, though, that any of them would refer to their burros in the way that Ramón Jiménez described Platero: "—so soft to touch that one would think he were all cotton, that he had no bones."

My soft-heartedness toward burros was not an asset in Spain, and later I felt uncomfortable when I talked with Gypsies in Vera in Almería province who bought old burros to sell to sausage makers in Barcelona.

I asked the old man if it were true that Gypsies got the better of Castilians when buying and selling. He chuckled. "You have to watch them. They can tie false tails to mules to change their appearance and dose a horse with arsenic to make its eyes shine."

George Borrow, in *The Bible in Spain*, has similar tales about Gypsies. One of them concerns a Castilian who complained that a Gypsy, when showing off a burro to him, whispered something in Caló to the animal that made him go through wonderful paces. But after the Castilian bought the burro, it threw him. I suspect these stories are mainly apocryphal.

In a nearby bar where I took my new acquaintance for a glass of wine, he told me about a knife battle, later confirmed by Falcó, between some Gypsies from Benalúa and Alcudia. It took place on the main street in front of a shop that sold guns and ammunition. "One Gypsy," he said, "died and several were wounded. The Guardia Civil detachment ran down from their quarters to stop the fight. They were too late."

"What caused it?" I asked.

"Honor," he replied. "A Gypsy woman from Benalúa. Her brother was killed defending her reputation."

While he gave me the details of the bloody encounter, I was reminded that voices of death, violent and brutal, often sound among the Gypsies of Spain. I was learning that it is not by chance that their dwindling vocabulary in Caló retains several violence-related words — all carried out of India: *churí* (knife), *chinelar* (to cut), *chingar* (to fight), and *mar* and *marelar* (to kill). Later, Gypsies would show me where they conceal their knives. Some put them inside their boots, others in especially-sewn pockets in trousers and coats.

During these early weeks in the city, in view of what Falcó, the old man and others had told me of the fierceness of the Guadix Gypsies, I reconsidered my objective in coming to Spain. Did I still want to get close to them? Was it prudent?

I had to accept the volatile nature of the Gypsies. The conflicts described to me had been among Gypsies, not between Gypsies and *payos*, so it might be that if I acted honorably as I went among them, my life would not be in danger. My decision, then, was to go ahead with my plan of getting acquainted with these Spanish outcasts. I realized that this would displease my Castilian friends, but while I valued their friendship Gypsies were my priority, not Castilians.

# 3

# Gypsies in the City

I hoped that the yellow-shirted Gypsy bootblack was not aware that I was following him, although he had shined my shoes once before. I had decided to be more aggressive in meeting Gypsies, and had made the bootblack my target. My plan was to get to know him as he shined my shoes, hoping that he would someday introduce me to the city of caves.

He was carrying his equipment under one arm from the Bar Molinillo, near the park, along the main street to the Plaza de Abastos, the enclosed market; then up Mira de Amescua, named after the dramatist of the Golden Age of Spanish literature and a native of Guadix. Before reaching the Hotel Comercio, he turned right onto the Calle Ancha to the Bar Dólar, then to the Plaza Mayor, planted with bright flowers. His next destination was the lyceum, the nearly defunct men's club, whose members sometimes had shoes to be shined. He then dropped down a flight of stairs to the portal of San Torcuato, the ancient entrance to the city, crossed the highway to the Bar Molinillo, his circuit completed.

It was another market day, the *Sábado*, and the Gypsies, with more exuberance than ever, were behaving as though Guadix were theirs.

The city had a festive air. It seemed that the entire population and most of the residents of the twenty pueblos in the region were in the city. There was much shaking of hands and drinking in the bars, which by nine o'clock were filled with male customers. The main street, the highway to Almería, was filled with local traffic — burros, motorcycles,

*Old Gypsy couple outside the indoor market where they pass their time during the morning hours.*

handcarts, automobiles — and with big trucks carrying fresh produce to Madrid from Almería, sixty miles to the south.

By 7:00 a.m. the Gypsy market workers had descended from their caves and were unloading produce at the Plaza de Abastos. At 8:00 a.m., when the first shoppers arrived on the streets, the bootblacks and lottery vendors dashed among them crying out for clients. Other Gypsies were delivering goods in hand carts.

I had seen keen-witted Faustino, the Gypsy knife-sharpener, drawing people around him whether or not they had knives to be sharpened. *Gitanas* were striding majestically into the city, and a group of *gitanos* (Gypsy men) sitting on the curbing in front of the indoor market, reminded me that Gypsies have the knack of relaxing, wherever they are. I once saw a group of them lying at their ease on the deck of the ferry boat on the overnight trip from Mallorca to Alicante as though they had been at sea all of their lives.

By evening there would be no Gypsies in the city except for those who descended from the caves to attend the cinema. The others stayed in the city of caves, the men drinking in the cave taverns, the women visiting their neighbors until the evening meal, around eleven. They avoided the nightly *paseo* in the park between nine and eleven when families and young couples stroll arm-in-arm. One reason was that male and female teenage Gypsies were forbidden by custom to be together, even in the company of their parents. Also, the *paseo* required the strollers to keep in step, foreign to Gypsy nature.

On the bootblack's next circuit, I was waiting for him in front of the Bar Dólar. When he was through with another customer, I strolled over to him and said, *"Hola! Quiere limpiar mis chapires?"* (Do you want to shine my shoes?) *Chapires* was Caló.

In a second, he was sitting on his stool and had placed my foot on the stand. He was an ordinary-looking Gypsy of about thirty with an olive-colored skin, a roundish Mediterranean head and thinning hair. Shorter than the average Gypsy, he also lacked the fierce mustache and graceful mannerisms of many Gypsies. He did, however, have the intense look of the Gypsy, often accompanied with quick turns of his head. There was little time to talk. As soon as he finished, he darted off in search of more business, but I felt that I had made progress.

I probably could have selected a more Gypsy-looking Gypsy as a target to get acquainted with, but his yellow shirt made him easy to identify. I might have cultivated Gypsy lottery vendors, but a sale with them lasted only a few seconds, hardly time to begin a conversation.

It was a hot summer day, so I strolled toward the park to relax in its coolness. As I walked along, I played a game of identifying Gypsies. They came in many sizes, shapes and colors. They were normally darker than the Castilians, often a deep shade of brown. They usually had black hair, and, except for Antonio and one or two others, retained a full head of hair into old age.

Several times when I was lulled into thinking in terms of Gypsies with fairly light complexions like Antonio, I would be jarred into reality on seeing a Gypsy with such a dark skin that he might have left India yesterday instead of a thousand years ago. Physical descriptions alone, though, do not prepare the visitor for the savage impression the Guadix Gypsies project through their restless movements and fierce, penetrating look.

The Gypsy men dressed like working men, avoiding the bright colors of the *gitanas*. But there were some differences. Only one Gypsy wore a beret, common among non-Gypsies. And Antonio and other Gypsies never wore the dark shirts and trousers of the workers. Since this was the day of the *Sábado*, men in their upper teens and early twenties wore high-heeled shoes, elaborate see-through shirts and modishly designed coats. Some had long sideburns and long hair.

Another reason for my going to the park was that out-of-town Gypsies whiled away time there awaiting buses to their destinations in Almería, Alicante or Granada. That day a pitiful looking group of Gypsies was sitting on benches and lying on the ground, using personal belongings, wrapped in blankets or pieces of cloth, as pillows. One of the women, who was breast-feeding her baby, had a walleye.

Another had an infected leg, wrapped in a dirty rag. A boy was pawing through the rubbish in a trash can.

A few days later, the bootblack shined my shoes again. He now realized that I had a special interest in him. Unsure of how to react, he lied to me about his name, which he said was Fernando. I later found that it was Antonio and that he was the husband of Isabel. He began his story with, "I have a *chuquel*, dog in Caló, so smart that when my wife needs groceries, she puts the things she needs on a piece of paper around its neck. The dog goes to the store. The grocer fills the order and the dog returns home with the groceries."

I said I'd like to see the dog. What I really wanted, of course, was to visit his cave and to meet his family. He replied noncommittally, so I did not push the matter. We had exchanged names, and I had told him something about myself.

Like other Guadijeños Antonio's Spanish was terrible. I am not a linguist, although my spoken Spanish and French are good enough to use in travel in either France or Spain. But it is one thing to use Spanish with an educated Spaniard in Madrid and another to talk with an Andalusian. Most people in Guadix, for example, do not pronounce final 's,' whether Gypsy or not. *Los gitanos* (the Gypsies) is pronounced as though written *lo gitano*. The city of Guadix is pronounced "Guaí."

During the next week or so, he shined my city shoes so frequently that I had to kick them in the dust to make them look as though they needed to be shined. I told Falcó that I called them my "Gypsy" shoes.

In a strange country, I usually give too much or too little for services that have no fixed price, whether for a porter in Paris or a Gypsy bookblack in Guadix. The first time Antonio shined my shoes, when I said to him, "*Cúanto vale?*" he simply shrugged his shoulders. I gave him ten pesetas, then worth about twenty American cents. He accepted the money without comment, but I later found that fifteen pesetas was the going price. If he shined twenty pairs of shoes a day, he would earn about three hundred pesetas, which that year was what a laborer earned per day. I doubt, though, that he had many twenty shoe-shine days.

With his Gypsy quickness, Antonio had sensed that through him I hoped to meet other Gypsies. He had turned this over in his mind for some time without letting me know. Later in our relationship, he told me he had wanted to introduce me earlier to the cave area, but had been discouraged by a Castilian from whom he asked advice, and who

*El golondrina, shoe-shine kit under his arm, crosses the highway to Almería toward the indoor market.*

had said, "It is not proper for a Gypsy to associate with a *señorito americano*."

Even though I was aware of the store owners' attitudes toward the Gypsies, it took a personal experience in which I embarrassed myself and Antonio to bring it home to me. I introduced Antonio to a school teacher, who had helped me become acquainted with the city and its history. To my chagrin, neither acknowledged the introduction. It was obvious that I had made a mistake in introducing a Gypsy to a middle-class Castilian. The teacher spoke only to me. Antonio, not to be out-done, stared off into space. This left me in the awkward position of talking to two people, each of whom ignored the other. Fortunately, this incident lasted only a few minutes. The teacher said *"adiós"* to me, still ignoring Antonio. I quickly gave him an *"adiós"* and one to Antonio, relieved that my lesson in middle-class Castilian rules of conduct toward Gypsies was finished for the day.

I couldn't anticipate it then, but despite this mishap and other false starts, I was entering a relationship with this bootblack that would lead to a warm friendship, and one that would give me an insight into the Gypsy world beyond my expectations. But after a few years a dark cloud—call it fate, if you will—beyond our control passed over us. It was to cause deep pain to me and to his wife and children, and was not to pass away until blood had been shed and one of the actors in the drama jailed. And even after the ritual bloodletting, our friend-ship was altered and years must pass before the wounds would heal. But all that was in the future.

I didn't have to go to the cave city to meet one of the most colorful Gypsies in the region, Juan. He worked in the Bar Dólar across from Falcó's shop.

"He has a nickname," Falcó said. "*El golondrina* (the swallow), and it suits him fine. He darts around the city like a bird on errands for clients of the bar where he's the Gypsy-in-residence. The bartenders and waiters get paid, but not Juan. To support his eight children, he relies on tips for his errands and shining shoes."

Falcó, despite his dislike of Gypsies, respected Juan. Perhaps it was because Juan showed no signs of inferiority because of the work he did and, through his erect carriage and soldierly walk, made it clear that the *payos* of the city of houses were no better than he. Somehow, he always managed to look debonair. In the winter, he wore a coat and vest with an ascot tie. As the weather got warmer, he shed his coat but retained the vest through most of the summer except in the hot weather of July and early August when he wore elaborately-styled shirts.

Cheerful and witty, Juan gestured broadly to illustrate his jokes. One day he burst into Falcó's shop, and, at attention, he stiffly saluted us. "I am now in the French Foreign Legion," he said. "What can I do for you?" He then whirled about and left. When a store owner asked him if he were worried about fragments of satellites falling on him he replied, "Not at all. I fear only snakes and *payos*." Once after my arrival in Guadix he ran to Falcó, shouting "He has come! He has come!" and raised his arms as though heralding the Saviour. In the late 1970s, as his shoe-shine business dwindled, he tried construction work. One day was enough. "That work," he said, "is for *payos*."

Juan and I often met on the city streets when he was running errands and would wave at each other or exchange a hurried handclasp. Knowing of my interest in Caló — I was trying to find out what still existed of the language — he would dart into a store where he had seen me, give me a word and be off. He introduced me to an old Castilian, a retired veterinarian, who knew more of the language than most Gypsies. He was the first person I met who still remembered the words for horse (*gras*), mare (*grañi*), straw (*pus*), and for fish (*machón*).

*Despite his dislike of Gypsies, Falcó the paper store owner was on good terms with the Gypsy* el Golondrina *of the Bar Dólar, and did not object to posing with him.*

Through Juan, I met a cobbler, an unlettered, hard-working man, whose shop was near the bar. I had been chatting with him for several weeks without any inkling he knew Caló until Juan told me.

"Juan tells me you speak Caló," I said to him.

"That's right. I like the language. I've learned it from the Gypsies."

He knew many words, and shared them with me while continuing with his work. We had a different learning process. I jotted down expressions new to me. He did not write, so he had to rely on his memory alone. At first, it seemed strange that the only non-Gypsy I had met in the city with an interest in Caló was this cobbler. But as I thought more about it, I realized that in a city where the businessmen, whose standards controlled the city, looked down on the Gypsies, their language would have no importance.

While I had been trying to further my relationship with Antonio the bootblack and to meet other Gypsies, unknown to me there had been a Gypsy in the hotel. I had noticed that my room was hardly being cleaned, so I spoke to the maid, whose name was Isabeth. She responded timidly, and for a few days there was a slight improvement. Sometime later, I noticed her chatting with two *gitanas* in the street. Something began to stir in the back of my head. Could it be that she was a Gypsy? She didn't look like one. She wasn't at all dark. In fact, her skin was fair, and she had naturally rosy cheeks. She was a pretty girl with even features and good teeth. Young and shy, she was perhaps seventeen. Her figure was short and trim; her breasts full. To me, the only indication that she might be a Gypsy was that she combed her hair straight back and caught it in the back of her head with a small red ribbon. But this wasn't an infalliable sign, because some Castilian women wore their hair in the same style—María the cook for example.

I had my answer a week or so later. By mid-afternoon one day, my bed hadn't been made. When I spoke to María and Miguel, they told me that Isabeth hadn't come to work that day. María said she would do my room, adding, "Isabeth is like all the Gypsies," thus letting me know that Isabeth was a Gypsy.

"What do you mean?" I asked.

"They don't like to work," she replied.

María, although a Castilian, looked more Gypsy than Isabeth. She told me that Isabeth had been working in the hotel only a short time, that she was married and had two small children. They thought that perhaps she or the children were ill—and that was why she hadn't come to work that day.

Now that I knew that Isabeth was a Gypsy, I began to observe her more carefully. It was obvious that her heart was not in her work. One day at mid-morning, while I was looking out of my window, I saw her standing on the balcony next to my room, dreamily gazing down onto the busy street watching the passersby, her thoughts far from her hotel duties. In this, she was not unlike other *gitanas* who worked in city houses and shops. None liked the work, and some wore a sullen expression, but not Isabeth. She dreamed the workday away, doing as little cleaning as possible. Unsuited by temperament to be a hotel maid, she eventually went back to her cave with her husband and children.

Frequent meetings with Antonio along the city streets and with Juan in and away from the Bar Dólar (and having talked with Isabeth), taught me more about Gypsies. Juan, like Faustino the knife sharpener, was the prototype Gypsy of Spanish literature. Bright, lively and jaunty, he could have stepped out of the pages of a story by Cervantes. Antonio had none of these qualities, but was not less of a Gypsy. I felt, though, that what I was seeing of them in the city was, in part, a mask with which they hid themselves to conceal their inner life from the residents of the city of houses. I could probably talk to them forever in the city without their revealing to me the secrets of their existence in the city of caves.

Since I could not wait indefinitely for Antonio to unlock the gates of that city—Juan had ignored my hints that I would like to go to *arriba* (up)—I determined to approach its outer limits, and to explore as much of its terrain as I could until forced to withdraw by its touchy inhabitants, whether Gypsy or non-Gypsy.

# 4

# The City of Caves

The clay hills that encompass it on
every side, are the most extraordinary
in nature. Whole villages are dug
into them.

TRAVELS THROUGH SPAIN (1777)
*Henry Swinburne*

One Sunday morning, during a solitary exploration along the periphery of the cave city, I had an eerie experience. I was strolling along the top of the ridge leading up from the church of Fátima. Bright, white chimneys from caves dug into the sides of the ridge jutted up through the earth around me. On the ancient stone-paved *era* below, a team of mules threshed wheat. Off to the right was the rounded back of the hill known as Cerro de la Bala, which I called the Gypsy mountain because just on the other side many Gypsies lived. A scattering of white chimneys and cave fronts led up to the base of its steep walls, which Gypsy and Castilian children climbed like mountain goats.

In the warm morning sun, I gradually became aware of religious music and the voice of a priest saying Mass. I turned around and looked back down at the church. It was too far away for the sound to carry to where I was standing. Also, there was no Mass being held. I started off again, puzzling over this strange occurrence. How was it possible for me to be hearing a Mass while I was walking alone outdoors? Then I understood. The sound was coming from the caves below. The residents were listening to a Mass on their television sets. The voice of the priest wafted to me through the chimneys. Since the chimneys were about six feet tall, it was as though the Mass were being broadcast from a series of loudspeakers on a level with my ears.

Near here, I had my first experience with one of the hazards strangers face who enter the cave area—harassment by children. An

English travel writer who visited Guadix wrote that wild coveys of wolfish slum children, who inhabited the caves, forced him to retreat headlong down the slopes. Even Jan Yoors, author of *The Gypsies*, who as a child among the Gypsies in Belgium witnessed Gypsy children fending off unwanted visitors, was defeated by them in his attempt to penetrate the city of caves.

I was walking along the base of the ridge where I had heard the sound of the Mass coming up through the chimneys. Suddenly a pack of five or six brown-faced boys with three skinny dogs, who had run down from the top of the ridge above, surrounded me. It was a classic Iberian attack on the intruder whether Greek, Carthagenian, Roman or American—and not unlike the Japanese banzai charges I once experienced. Although these warriors were only ten to twelve years old, and their uniforms consisted only of raggedy shorts, they were, nonetheless, an effective force—an abundant supply of loose stones was at their disposal.

"*Un duro! Un duro!*" they shouted as they darted around me holding out their hands. (A duro is equal to five pesetas, worth at that time about ten cents.)

This was a critical moment. I was being tested. Not only were the boys awaiting my reaction, but so were the residents of the nearby caves. I had no idea what to do, but I did not want to give money under duress. Neither did I want to retreat, so I decided to take the initiative.

"Where are you going?" I asked.

To my relief, this was the right approach. They said they were on the way to swim in a nearby irrigation ditch. I continued with my questions in a joking kind of way:

"How old are you?"

"How many brothers and sisters do you have?"

"Where do you live?"

They enjoyed talking about themselves and their families, and answered all of my questions. I told them that I was an American interested in their city and their caves. As a final question, I asked them which ones were Gypsies. They were all so brown they looked alike, but I felt that some of them must be Gypsies. Three boys pointed at two of the others who, with big smiles, nodded their heads and said, "We are pure Gypsies."

"I knew it," I replied. "You beg better."

They all laughed with bright teeth shining, and then, arms waving back at me, they scurried off for their swim, shouting, "*Adiós! Adiós!*"

A few weeks after the encounter, I was walking among the caves with a Castilian from the city below. We approached a small, level area surrounded by cones of earth in which caves had been dug. The air was full of dust, kicked up by boys playing soccer. Some of the players looked familiar, and I must have looked familiar to them. Was one of them waving his arms at me? He seemed to be, so I waved back. It brought an immediate response. The boy, followed by the others, came bounding toward me, shouting, "*Americano! Americano!*" To the relief of my Castilian friend, who had been wondering about the purpose of the charge, the boys only wanted to welcome me. After grasping my hand and looking up at me with dirty, happy faces, they hurried back to their game, followed by the usual pack of skinny dogs.

I had made several discoveries here. One was that Gypsy and non-Gypsy children play together. Perhaps not much of a discovery, but it wasn't known in the city of houses below where I had been told that children of the two races never played together, even if their families lived in adjacent caves. I also learned something about myself. My reaction to their assault was reassuring. I had enjoyed the experience. I liked these untamed children, and they seemed to like me. A dividend was that the boys in later meetings shared their detailed knowledge of cave life with me. And having learned that they responded well to directness, I used the same technique successfully with adults. "How old are you?" I would ask. "Where do you work?" "How many children do you have?" In exchange, I willingly answered questions about myself.

Approaching Gypsy dwelling places is always precarious, though. A few years later when I carelessly entered as a stranger the Polígono del Sur barrio on the outskirts of Seville, where most of the city's Gypsies now live, a Gypsy teenager tried to jerk my camera away.

The breakthrough in my relationship with Antonio, which led to my introduction to the cave city, came a few weeks later. I was driving back to Guadix from a day in the city of Baza, thirty miles to the east on the road to Murcia. After passing the railroad station, which is on the outskirts of Guadix, I saw Antonio walking on the side of the road. He looked hot, as though he had been working, but he was far from his shoe-shine circuit. When I came abreast of him, I waved. He returned my greeting and then shouted, "Stop." I stopped and he got into the car.

"I've been working on a beer truck, taking the place of a friend who is sick," he said.

"Do you want a lift up to the cave area?" I asked.

"*Está bien. Vámono!*"

Going up the street past my hotel, we came to the lovely church of Santiago, its baroque front recently restored. Here the street became narrow, perhaps twelve feet wide, just room for my small European car to pass. It was paved with brick and stone — not with the asphalt of below. Pedestrians constantly spilled over into the street because the sidewalks were so narrow that only one person at a time could negotiate them.

"Sound your horn!" said Antonio. "Let people know you are coming so they can get onto the sidewalk."

In another hundred yards, we came to a plaza-like area, the Cruz de Piedra, where we turned right at the base of the high, ochre wall of the Arab fortress, now a seminary. Several spacious cave homes, still occupied, had been dug into the wall many years ago. We soon were on Calle San Miguel which led directly into the cave complex. The road became an unmarked track, with the driver free to pick his own way. Antonio directed me to drive beyond several caves where there was a level spot for parking.

"Do you want to see more of the caves?" he asked.

This was what I had been anticipating. I said that I did — hoping that he would take me to his cave. He then led me along a poorly defined route toward a mountain-like pass between two jagged peaks. The cool, early evening breeze of mid-summer blew the dust away that our feet kicked up. In the winter and spring, the trail would be muddy and we would slip and slide before getting to the top of the pass.

"Antonio," I said, "this is my first visit to the center of the cave area."

"What do you think of it?" he asked.

"Wonderful!" I replied, as I looked at the lunar-like landscape, almost devoid of trees and grass.

Antonio nodded his head. He was familiar with the reaction of foreigners, who sometimes paid to visit the cave city.

It was difficult to conceive of man living in this wasted terrain of stark, yellow-brown conical peaks in which the caves were dug. It reminded me on a smaller scale of big mountains, such as the Italian Dolomites, that I had climbed.

"Let's stop for a minute," I said to Antonio. "I want to look around a little."

Far below, I could see the most prominent landmarks in the city of houses: the Arab fortress, the cathedral and the new apartment houses.

Beyond them were the river bed and the escarpment of the plateau on the other side of the river. But we were in another city, a city of caves, spread over an area larger than the city proper; it had its own cave-stores and bars and churches. Without streets, except for a paved road leading to one of the churches, the Ermita Nueva, its six thousand residents for the most part came and went on foot although small automobiles and motorcycles could negotiate some of the trails.

What from a distance had appeared to be a sterile landscape devoid of life, now showed a constant flow of activity: children playing, mothers sweeping clean the earth in front of their caves and hanging clothes out to dry, chickens scratching, burros and mules swishing their tails and braying and even cows in cave-barns.

Two brown-faced Gypsy boys scurrying home to their caves, on seeing me, shouted, *"Francés! Francés! "* (Frenchman! Frenchman!) Like the other children, they assumed I was French because I was a foreigner. A generation ago, they might have used *franchute* as in *"Viene aquí un franchute*! (Here comes a Frenchman!)

Continuing along the narrow trail, we rounded a sharp curve and came on a Gypsy in his twenties sharpening a knife in front of his cave home. I tried not to stare as we walked by — Antonio greeted him with a muted *"Hola"* — but found it difficult not to, because of what I had seen in the city below. I reminded myself again that while I could not shrug off the Gypsies' use of knives to settle disputes, I was hoping to find a more balanced view of Gypsy life than the one availble to the residents of the city of houses.

Then, two Castilian men came striding briskly along leading two white burros, one laden with grass, the other with a sack of potatoes. The grass, freshly cut along the river bed, would be the burros' supper. Farther down the trail, a brown mule was pulling a melon-laden two-wheeled cart with green sides and rubber tires. Behind the mule, two cows pulled a high-wheeled wagon loaded with wood. A motorcyclist zoomed down a steep ridge on a ready-made motocross course. Two emaciated dogs, that looked like starving greyhounds, barked loudly at us from a nearby cave. "Don't worry about them," said Antonio. "They are cowards." I appreciated Antonio's reassurance, but was later nipped by a cave dog.

Dogs, along with children, are among the guardians of the cave city. They make up the first line of defense. Dogs sense the stranger at once, probably by the way he walks and by his odor. Both Gypsies and non-Gypsies own them. Once, when I was being harassed by a dog

*The giant cave chimneys dominate the terrain of the city of caves.*

belonging to a Castilian, it was a *gitana* who had the owner call off the dog.

Around us, jutting up from caves below the earth to a height of six or seven feet, were the magnificent chimneys of Guadix. They are truly an art form, unsurpassed in the rest of Spain or in the south of Portugal, where the houses also have attractive chimneys. In other cave-dwelling communities, chimneys are taken for granted and are often meager little things, maintained just enough to prevent them from tumbling down. But the chimneys of Guadix receive careful attention from their proud owners who keep them glistening with whitewash. Their shapes vary. Some are round and some are four sided. The caps, which have draft holes in them, can be either circular, pointed or squared. While most chimneys spring unannounced from the earth, where they stand like sentinels, a few have been molded into the exterior of cave walls and look like pieces of sculpture. As for the caves, few of the ones I visited elsewhere were as well constructed.

I never saw a chimney or a cave being constructed, because no new caves had been dug for the past twenty years or so, ever since the residents began to emigrate to Barcelona. But there was nothing complicated about their construction.

"I helped dig them when I was a boy," said Antonio. "We sliced off a knoll and then cut into the face to make the cave rooms. The first room is often the kitchen, but it can also be a living room, or perhaps an entranceway with other rooms off it."

Stepping into an abandoned cave, I saw that each of the four rooms had a rounded ceiling about eight feet high with several feet of earth above it for a roof. Walls between rooms were three feet thick. One room had a tiled floor; the others brick. The number of rooms and the floor plan depended on the shape of the knoll. Larger caves had seven or eight rooms. A few had windows, and some had two stories. Later, I visited an unoccupied cave of three stories, with inside earthen steps leading to each floor.

By the mid to late 1970s, the selling prices of caves reflected the arrival of inflation in Spain. Good caves, which sold for a few hundred dollars in the 1960s, were worth two or three thousand dollars. Antonio pointed to a cave with a well, a fenced-in yard and an inside flush toilet that had just sold for five thousand dollars.

There is nothing monotonous in the arrangement of the caves of Guadix—no mid-20th century sub-division of houses, all in a line, with neatly cropped lawns facing the street. They are located wherever there is a convenient hillock for excavating. Some are side-by-side, others are on top of one another (sometimes up to four levels). This means that the chimney of one cave protrudes up through the front yard of the cave above it. No two caves are alike. Next to us was a miserable dwelling with its front badly in need of whitewash. But just below it was a noble creation with a soaring, rectangular facade about twenty feet long and twenty feet high. A little higher was a cave whose owners had erected a high wall in front with red-capped posts and an iron gate enclosing a garden with a grape vine, peppers, tomatoes and flowers. Its one window had venetian blinds. Another cave had an exterior room. "It's a *casa-cueva* (house-cave)," Antonio told me.

Generally, the cave exteriors are in the shape of squares and rectangles, but I have seen caves whose curved facades and protruding side walls created forms not recognizable to Euclidean geometry.

"The best caves," Antonio said, "are low in the cave area. They have more rooms. The soil around them is better for growing flowers

*The City of Caves with its jumble of cave homes, placed wherever a hillock or ravine wall is available for excavating, is too complex for the visitor to comprehend.*

and vegetables, and they are closer to the city shops."

On another visit Antonio showed me an entire ravine lined with caves, forsaken, he said, by poor Castilians. I looked into some of them. They had been pitiful homes. Of only two or three rooms each, and of inferior construction, their roofs and walls had tumbled in. They reflected the poverty of their former owners.

"These people," Antonio said, "ate the dead mules and burros which were buried at the head of the ravine."

"Where did these dead animals come from?" I asked.

"From the city below. This was their burial ground."

When I was a boy in Massachusetts, my father showed me where horses from the town were once buried. The site was full of mounds, grown over with grass. No one had ever lived there, though.

In 1970 the city government, trying to put some order to the jumble of caves, assigned each cave a number according to the traditional name of the barrio where it was located. It was still difficult, however, to reach an accurate figure on how many were occupied. One city official estimated two thousand, but after talking with cave dwellers and mailmen whose routes included the caves, I came up with a figure of eleven or twelve hundred.

One of the disadvantages to cave living is the possibility of the earthen roof collapsing. Except for good fortune, my wife and I might have been casualties in the village of Cuevas de Almanzora in Almería province. The morning we arrived, the long summer drought had been broken by a torrential rain, which forced away great blocks of earth from a cliff face, crushing several caves burrowed into its base, and burying three Gypsies. Later that day, while visiting a chapel above the cliff face, I almost backed our car into a gaping crevasse left by the same slide that had engulfed the caves.

In the cave city of Guadix, though, with the favorable mix of clay, sandstone and other soils, accidents seldom occur, but in the village of Fonelas, where the soil is not as good, several families in recent years have suffered losses from roofs falling in.

"How old are the caves?" I asked Antonio.

"Very old," was the reply. He only knew that they must be old because his grandparents had lived there, but Carlos Asenjo, a local historian, has found that the first caves were built in the 1500s to house an expanding population. By the 1600s there were four hundred caves.

Antonio had no idea when the first Gypsies came to Guadix, and didn't care. It seems likely, though, that they arrived not long after the city surrendered to Ferdinand and Isabella in 1489—as they did in Granada where they were living in the early 1500s. They have long been aware of the advantages of city living. An Englishman in 1817 noted a common Gypsy saying, "Money is in the city, not in the countryside." Other Gypsies, though, continued their nomadic existence for hundreds of years. On large scale maps of the region, I discovered topographic features, mostly in the mountains, long forgotten locally, that go back to a time when Gypsies controlled some of the routes in and out of the region.

| | |
|---|---|
| Collado de la gitana | Pass of the Gypsy<br>(4,000 ft.) |
| Cuerda de los gitanos | Range of the Gypsies |
| Cortijo del caló | The Gypsy farm |

From where we were standing, Antonio pointed in the direction of his cave. "It is in the *barrio* of Cañada Ojeda," he said. "That is where most Gypsies live, but we also have caves in Cañada Gracia and other barrios."

On seeing non-Gypsies walking toward Antonio's barrio, I asked him if Castilians also lived there. He replied, "Yes, many do."

This was another discovery. Even Spanish authors did not know that the two races live side-by-side—or perhaps they preferred not to. A book recently published in Spain on Andalusia referred to the quarter as "*Las cuevas de los gitanos.*" To make it more confusing, even non-Gypsies who live there sometimes call it *Barranco de los gitanos* (Ravine of the Gypsies). My first reaction was one of disappointment that the "savage" Gypsies of Guadix did not live by themselves in a mountain retreat, expelling non-Gypsies, guarding their Romany language and, perhaps, ruled by a tribal chief or at least a *phuri dai* (matriarch). But as I continued to think about it, I realized that the Gypsies' living closely with Castilians made all the more remarkable their remaining Gypsies.

"I'm going to take a few pictures," I said to Antonio, and climbed up to a platform in front of an abandoned cave where I was almost trapped by one of the ever-present dangers of cave life, a hole, fifteen feet deep, left when the chimney of a ruined cave underneath had collapsed. These chimney holes, some three feet in diameter, are large enough for an adult to fall into. Unfortunately, only a few are filled, although some thoughtful cave dwellers stuff loose branches into them to warn the unwary. Another danger on the platform was the broken glass, great chunks of it, sharp enough to cut through my shoes. Human feces were liberally distributed about.

As I looked down on the city below, I saw that houses and caves were separated by an irregular line. The poet from Barcelona called it "the imaginary frontier" that separates the *cueveros* from *los de abajo* (the people below). I tried out the poet's concept on an old priest with whom I was drinking coffee in the Bar Dólar. He agreed with the poet's idea, adding, "But it's not imaginary. It's very real. There is a world of difference between the cave residents and the inhabitants of the city of houses. The *cueveros* are considered to be of a lower class."

Miguel the waiter put it succinctly when he said that *los de las cuevas* (the people from the caves) are "*afuera de la ciudad.*" (outside of the city.) The names given to the people below by the cave dwellers are *los señoritos* and *la gente bien.* (people of the upper class.)

The separation also affects urban services to the cave city. The city provides them with two schools, electricity and potable water outlets (electricity for many years; potable water since 1969). But for many other services, the cave dwellers are ignored. I never saw a policeman on patrol, although I did in the cave areas of some of the villages. The worst oversights, though, are the lack of garbage and trash collection, and the absence of help in the disposal of human waste.

Antonio said that some inhabitants never left the cave area to descend into the city below. I think he was exaggerating, but it was possible to live there indefinitely. Fresh bread was delivered daily by bicycle and tiny trucks from bakeries below. The men had a choice among twenty-five taverns in which they could spend their evenings. For the religious, there were two churches, one of them in a cave.

Antonio, becoming bored with my long-winded photography on the shelf above him, began to sing irritably in a poor voice:

*Somos los pobres gitanos*
*más pobres que las alondras.*
We are poor Gypsies
poorer than the larks.

So, taking one last photograph, I descended from my outlook and rejoined Anonio who said, *"adiós,"* before continuing up the trail leading to his cave, leaving me to descend to my car alone. He wasn't quite prepared to take me to his cave home.

Although I knew the caves were not inhabited by Gypsies alone, I thought of Lorca's imaginary city of the Gypsies, which once viewed could not be forgotten. It is a city of the poet's fancy—of pain and towers of cinnamon—whose inhabitants live, love and die and are persecuted by their traditional enemy, the Guardia Civil. The cave city of Guadix, although it had cinnamon towers and sorrows, was not an imaginary city. It was a city of real people, who guarded their privacy, sallying forth in the morning to work and to shop, and returning in the early evening to their cave bars and cave homes. Through my guide Antonio, I was becoming familiar with this unusual city, and with his continued help I hoped to become acquainted with its residents.

# 5

# Initiation into the Gypsy World

The miserable peasantry dwell
in holes or cuevas excavated
from soft hillocks.

HANDBOOK FOR SPAIN (1845)
*Richard Ford*

A few days after our visit to the cave city, Antonio was shining my shoes in front of the Bar Dólar.

"I have a baby she-goat. Do you want to see her?" he asked.

Of course I was eager to visit his cave and to meet his family. We arranged to see each other at the bar at eight that night. Antonio didn't say night, though. He said, *"Ocho de la tarde,"* which literally translates as eight in the afternoon. I always had to wrestle mentally with this use of *tarde*, because it extended until nine p.m., not the usual five p.m. to which I was accustomed. When I went to the bar that evening, I wondered if he would have a different concept of time than mine. He didn't. He had an accurate wrist watch, and let me know that I was a few minutes late.

We drove to the edge of the cave city where I parked. Antonio then led me over the pass we had earlier climbed, and descended toward the bottom of another valley lined with caves. The sound of flamenco burst from one of them. The path led along a high brick wall that enclosed a factory for making clay water jugs. The potter's wheel was in a cave in which the family had its living quarters. After a few minutes of climbing out of the valley, Antonio, pointing to the white-washed exterior of a cave dug into a sharp ridge, said, "My cave."

In front of it was a kind of dirt plaza with a spigot for supplying the several caves around it. The group of caves made up one of the many neighborhoods in the city of caves. They were thirty-five to seventy feet apart and had been excavated at various times during the past several hundred years.

Antonio walked to the cave nearest his, shouting, *"Hola! Hola!"* Several people came tumbling out. One plump Gypsy woman in her thirties had a fair, rosy skin, and crafty-looking eyes which made me distrust her. Her husband, a lame non-Gypsy, unshaven and unkempt, stood beside her. (He was the only Castilian in the region, male or female, married to a Gypsy.) They made their living selling lottery tickets. The *gitana*, Rosa, ran up to me, boldly taking hold of my arms.

*"Baile! Baile!"* she cried.

And moving her hips in what was supposed to be flamenco, she offered to dance for me—for a fee. I politely declined. She accepted my refusal, but pushing forward her five-year old *chaborí*, a beautiful girl, she encouraged her to perform. "Dance! Dance for the señor!" So the little girl, assuming the pose of the flamenco dancer—one hand above her head and the other on her hip—danced a few steps and then stopped, holding out her hand for money.

"Come on," said Antonio leading me to the next dwelling a few yards away, but up a steep path. Five or six old, poorly-dressed Gypsies were sitting in front of the cave, some on the ground, others on chairs. Their poverty was obvious, but they asked nothing from me. "She is my mother-in-law," said Antonio, pointing to a woman in her early sixties. Tall and lean, she was a fine-looking woman with noble, aquiline features. She carried herself proudly and erectly, feet firmly planted on the ground, and hands on hips, Gypsy fashion. Later, when we became better acquainted, she offered to wash my trousers, soiled from the hands of Antonio's children. She also asked me to take photographs of herself with her best friend, who with her brown complexion and wrinkled face, looked to be a twin. When I told Falcó about this, he said, "Ah! This is significant. Gypsies usually ask money for photographs. You are gaining their confidence."

As we approached the next cave, I heard pigs snorting, and when Antonio opened the wooden gate in front of the fenced-in yard, I saw two huge boars, three sows and about twenty piglets in pens. The Castilian couple who lived there raised hogs for a living. He was serious-faced but hospitable. Lean from hard work and short, he always wore a felt hat. His wife was sturdily built with the weathered and wrinkled skin of a person who has worked out-of-doors most of her life. Like most non-Gypsy women, she was always in black. Jovial and outgoing, she had a twinkle in her eyes. "Antonio is a good neighbor," she said. "We love his children."

On the other side of the plaza was a cave with a high wall in front.

*This non-Gypsy, cave-dwelling neighbor of Antonio, along with her husband, has a successful pig-raising business.*

A middle-aged non-Gypsy couple lived there with their daughter, an attractive girl of sixteen with a cream-like complexion and jet black hair. When Antonio took me behind their wall, they were sitting in the shade of a large tree, one of the few in the neighborhood. It was the time of the mini-skirts, and the daughter was wearing one, but over a pair of long slacks for modesty. The father, a grave individual, who worked at odd jobs, always wore a black beret. His wife was shy, round-faced, short and robust. They proudly showed me through their seven-room cave. It was clean, neat and attractively furnished. They offered me a glass of water from their well and said it was seventy-five feet deep and never ran dry. Antonio, using the Caló word for water, assured me that it was pure. "*Es un pañí muy puro.*" He was right; it was sweet and cool. I drank two glasses. (Up until 1969 when the city water system was revamped, the water from the cave wells was purer than that of the city below which had a high typhoid and paratyphoid content.)

"Did you notice?" Antonio asked later of the non-Gypsy, "he did not offer you a glass of wine. He should have, but he is not generous."

While we were talking with the family, a bronze Gypsy amazon walked majestically past the cave. She was not wearing shoes. "It is Concha," said Antonio. "She is the widowed sister of my wife." The black, shapeless, knee-length dress she was wearing did little to conceal her voluptuousness. She must have looked like the *gitana* described by Ramón Jiménez whose coppery nakedness overflowed inside her rags. I thought of her as a Gypsy queen, the queen of the city of caves, for she rarely descended to the city below. She was one of those cave dwellers who preferred to spend most of her life high above the city's crowded streets where there was always a breeze and a view of distant horizons — and freedom from conflict with the dwellers of the city below.

On the few occasions when she did enter the city of houses, she continued to wear black — in memory of her husband. Even her shoes and stockings were black. But from the neck up, she was not in mourning. Silver earrings matched a silver comb set high on her head. On her temples, she arranged her coal black hair into *caracoles* (spit curls) with a tightly braided pony tail falling to her shoulders.

Later, when she spoke to me in Antonio's cave, her voice was soft and subdued, but her deep, brown eyes, at once fierce and sensuous, spoke more clearly of her inner self than did her spoken words. When I was in her presence, I dared not look into her bold eyes for fear of betraying my interest in her. I suppose that it was just as well that I chose this course. Otherwise, her brothers would likely have flashed their knives. But assuming they had no objections, could I have lived with Concha? Perhaps earlier in my life, but not now. Her world was too far from mine. Although I was becoming close to the Gypsies, and although they sometimes mistook me for one of them because of my Caló, I had one foot planted in another world where my wife and family lived.

One day I observed the wild, explosiveness of Concha's character. I had climbed to the top of Cerro de la Bala, and was sitting peacefully in the sun when suddenly I heard women's voices coming up from below. Walking to the edge of the summit plateau, I looked down in the direction of the sound. Two *gitanas*, standing on a narrow ridge, were arguing. One of them was Concha who was fiercely berating the other. The quarrel reached its climax when Concha made the sign of the cross with a stick on the ground to increase the power of the curse she was about to make, and then angrily strode away after screaming at her opponent, *"Malos chuqueles te jaman!"* (May evil dogs eat you!)

Although hardly a mile from the center of the city of houses, the city seemed to be light years away. But Antonio's cave was real, with its white front, almost twenty feet high, flush with the cut-away face of the earthen ridge. The top edge projected out about a foot and was covered with two layers of red tile to drain off rain water. The façade was covered with whitewash to prevent erosion.

Antonio went to an outbuilding and opened a gate. Out jumped Matilda, the baby goat, bleating for her supper. She shared her coop with several chickens, a duck and two rabbits. Many residents of the region—not just cave dwellers—kept animals and fowl as a source of food because most of them could not afford to buy meat in the market. Matilda, though, was being raised for milking, not eating.

An unusual feature of Antonio's cave was the two windows which an earlier tenant had cut into the cave front—few caves have windows. His windows had strong iron bars and wooden shutters.

"*No hay policía arriba*," (No police up here,) he explained. "At night I shut off the entrance to the cave with a wooden door, and lock it with this key," he said, pointing to an old-fashioned key which dangled from his belt. "And I secure it on the inside with a strong wooden bar."

A green cloth hung over the doorway of the cave to keep out the ever-present flies of Andalusia and the fierce summer sun. Antonio held open the cloth and beckoned for me to enter. It was dark inside, until he pulled the string of a light bulb hanging from the eight foot high ceiling.

We were standing in a small foyer with a clean floor of brick tile. Archways separated the rooms. Antonio motioned for me to go through one of them into the kitchen, where he prepared Matilda's meal, mixing powdered milk and water on the kitchen table. Matilda couldn't wait, and in a quick, dainty leap, she was on top of the table, nuzzling the milk carton. Antonio spanked her and she leaped back to the floor. He then warmed the milk on a two-burner butane stove which set against the wall under the big open chimney—he no longer used wood as a fuel.

I sat down on a cane chair and looked around the room. There was no running water, so the family had to carry it from the spigot in the plaza. The walls were painted blue, and the ceiling was shining from a recent application of whitewash applied to prevent the earth from crumbling. Several copper pots and pans were hanging on the wall, typical of Andalusia where copper utensils are used as decorations. Two hams and some peppers were strung from hooks in the ceiling. Later I found out that this kitchen was better equipped than those in many Gypsy caves, some of which still lacked stoves. Once while walking along a ridge, honeycombed with caves, I came upon a *gitana* cooking outside over a wood fire. With her disheveled clothing and bare feet, she could have been one of the Gypsies who entered Spain in the 1400s.

Antonio improvised a funnel of cardboard to pour the heated milk into Matilda's bottle. Then, while nursing Matilda, he said in a pensive manner, "You know, you are the first foreigner to visit my cave."

Soon I heard voices. Antonio's wife and children had arrived. His wife was a tall, handsome woman with a chocolate complexion, a strong-boned oval face and a high forehead, prominent eyebrows and evenly spaced white teeth. Her only pieces of jewelry were one ring and pendant earrings worn through pierced ear lobes. She had a demure, almost child-like look, but I was to find later that this was only one of her expressions. In a fraction of a second, this demureness could change into a fierce rage.

"*Es mi romí*," said Antonio nonchalantly, using the Caló word for wife, but without bothering to mention her name. Only later did I learn it was Isabel.

The five-year old boy at her side had a skin of a deeper brown than his mother. It was a hot day so he was wearing only underpants — some days he went naked. He was a bright boy with sparkling black eyes and an appealing personality.

"What's your name?" I asked.

"José," he replied.

We soon became friends and I called him Joselito.

Isabel was carrying a chubby, happy-looking baby boy about two years old. Named after his father, he was called Toñito. He was half-naked, but for my benefit was soon scrubbed and completely dressed in an un-Gypsy way. He did not look at all Gypsy. His face was fair, lighter than his parents, and his curly hair was brown. One of Isabel's sisters called him a *payo*, because of his light skin.

José took it on himself to show me through the rest of the cave, leading me first to the family living room, where he pointed with pride to a television set, two easy chairs and a sofa. On the walls was a print of the Virgin of Sorrows along with family photographs. One of them was of Antonio, taken during his military service. Gypsies, like other Spanish males, perform obligatory service. A sixteenth century saying, referring to undesirables not wanted by the Army, is no longer valid. "*No gitanos, no murcianos y demás gente de mal vivir.*" (No Gypsies, no one from Murcia, or other evil people.) Antonio's service did not change his attitude toward being a Gypsy. He returned to Guadix, married Isabel, and continued to live like a Gypsy.

"More," said José with his dark eyes shining, and taking me by the hand led me back through the kitchen into the master bedroom, which had a double bed, pillows, bedspread and blanket. It was plain that

Antonio and Isabel wanted the same comforts as their poor non-Gypsy neighbors.

Later, I found that Gypsies elsewhere in Spain shared this desire. En route to Barcelona, I stopped in the city of Totana in Murcia province where a Gypsy took me to his new house, which like Antonio's had a television, a cook stove and new furniture. He had earned the money for his purchases in Switzerland.

His wife, in her 50s, said to me, "There was much misery before. Now we can live like Castilians, yet remain Gypsies."

I hasten to point out that while many Gypsies shared in the improved Spanish economy of the 1960s and 1970s, others have remained poor and live in shanty towns such as the one in Conil on the road from Algeciras to Cádiz. But how could the family of a Gypsy bookblack afford to buy the new household furnishings I had seen? The answer was that Isabel worked part time as a cleaning woman in the city. But it was Antonio's responsibility to support the family. How different

*Isabel, Antonio's wife, pregnant in this photograph, mopped the cement slab in front of her cave daily.*

this was from the Gypsies I knew in the United States where the groom's family pays a bride-price of several thousand dollars to the bride's family, and a young Gypsy with a wife skilled in fortune telling can look forward to a life of ease.

Antonio and Isabel were amused when I told them about this custom. "Not for us," they said.

I asked Falcó what effect the Gypsies owning television sets and other luxury goods would have on them. "They will never change," he replied. "They will always be Gypsies."

"They will remain Gypsies as long as they think of themselves as Gypsies," I said. "Antonio feels no less a Gypsy because he has living room furniture, but if there will always be Gypsies, what about cave dwellers? Will the *cueveros* leave their homes?"

"Not for many years. Look at the advantages they have. No taxes. Maintenance costs are low. About the only need for cash outlay is to buy materials to mix whitewash to apply to the interior rooms and to the façade. The cave is protected from the wind and rain by the natural earth, so there are no heating bills."

We hadn't, though, mentioned one of the disadvantages to cave life, the lack of toilet facilities. The wooden privy of my New England youth was absent—I don't ever remember having seen one in southern Spain. Because of the lack of trees and underbrush on the barren knolls, privacy is a problem. Abandoned caves are often used. (Ruined churches, as I observed in the city of Lorca to the east, served as public conveniences, but not in Guadix.) A stranger entering a cave area must be on the alert to avoid interrupting the residents who need privacy. My technique was to whistle a tune to give a warning of my approach.

María, the cook, emphasized another drawback when I visited her in her cave home when she was ill. "We have no refuse collection, although the city below does. We have to get rid of our garbage and trash by ourselves. Some untidy people throw it outside their cave entrance, but most of us try to get it out of sight."

I wondered why it didn't spread disease, but I never heard of any epidemics, perhaps because of the dry air and warm sun of Andalusia.

Life around a Gypsy cave is an exciting experience, particularly for the children who live in a world of delight. It is not a make-believe world of toys and stuffed animals, but one throbbing with everyday life. It is filled with pigs and goats to be fed, roosters and hens to chase, burros and mules to watch and listen to as they bray, dogs to pet and children of all ages to play with. The non-Gypsy children share in this life, as well, but the Gypsy children have the best of it, because they have more freedom. They go naked and roll in the dirt, although Isabel scrubbed hers at least once a day.

Toñito, Antonio's and Isabel's two-year old, was a typical Gypsy child. He usually ran about naked. Sometimes, Gypsy fashion, he would be bottomless, wearing only a top which, depending on the weather, might be a cotton undershirt or a woolen sweater. My guess is that a child who goes bottomless is better off than one who is swathed in diapers. He is not going to be exposed to diaper rash.

Toñito was permitted liberties that my children never had. One evening when I was having dinner in the cave, I had just put to one side the sharp family knife after having used it to cut off portions of a melon. Toñito, who was standing next to the table, reached up, took the knife into his hands to cut his own melon. My first thought was to take the knife away, but thinking that his parents hadn't noticed his action, I asked,

"*El puede usar el churí?*" (Can he use the knife?)

The response was a nod of the head from Isabel.

Another day as I was climbing up the three steps leading out of the cave, Toñito was leaving at the same time. I started to take him by the hand to help him as I would have done with one of my own children at that age. But Joselito, who came along at that moment, held my hand back saying matter of factly, "Let him do it himself." And so I did—and Toñito, struggling as though climbing the north face of the Matterhorn, succeeded in getting out of the cave without help from anyone.

With this kind of encouragement, Gypsy children mature rapidly. Joselito, like Toñito, was already advanced for his age compared with other children I have known. He could ride a bicycle, take care of the neighbor's hogs and avoid the dangers of the open holes left when abandoned chimneys and cave roofs collapsed.

Isabel and other Gypsy mothers did not let their children climb the steep cliffs of the cave area, use sharp knives, and go naked because they lacked interest in them. They loved them and smothered them with kisses. They were aware of the uniqueness of their manner of raising children, and were convinced that it was superior to the non-Gypsy approach. One night in the cave when I said in front of Isabel and her mother that the Gypsy *chaborós* seemed to be healthier look-ing than children in the city of houses, they excitedly exclaimed,

"*Chachipé! Chachipé!* (True! True!) It is better for them to go naked than to wear diapers. Our *chaborós* play better and are stronger than the *payo* children."

I was delighted when, after several visits to the cave, Isabel asked if I would like to stay for dinner. It was already eleven o'clock at night, and Antonio and I had been sitting around the kitchen table drinking wine, eating fresh tomatoes spiced with hot sauce, chunks of bread and small pieces of garlic.

"I'm glad you like *gromanje* (tomatoes) and *manró* (bread)," said Isabel, using some Caló. "The meal will be simple."

She went about preparing our dinner on the two-burner butane stove. It was a great improvement over the wood and charcoal fires that her mother had to use. But it had disadvantages. It was so low that she had to bend over throughout her cooking, and one evening her face and neck were badly burned from spattering oil. She first fried potatoes and then some eggs—and quickly sliced cucumbers, peppers and tomatoes for a salad. Along with bread and wine, this was our meal. We ate the bread without butter or margarine. For dessert, we had watermelon. Isabel never made *flan* (custard), a staple item in my hotel, and never served sweets or bakery goods.

In the fall and winter, she bought pears and apples. Sometimes in the summer, she brought home a sack of prickly pears, known as *higochumbres* for the family to peel and eat. Tomatoes and peppers were available the year round. The family liked fish and ate it at least once a week. It was plentiful in the market where it was delivered early every morning from Almería. *Merluza* (hake), which I used to eat in my boyhood, was the fish most commonly eaten.

Isabel's menu, however, had its drawbacks. The morning cup of coffee was filled with sugar, and on those special occasions when the family drank hot chocolate, it, too, was thick with sugar.

I never asked Antonio and Isabel if they ate meat from dead animals, that is, from animals that had died of disease or old age as opposed to being slaughtered, for Isabel cooked nothing but the freshest of foods. Yet, this belief—often known as *mulo mas*—that the Gypsies of the world eat dead animals is widespread. A government official in Guadix said to me, "Several years ago a family of Gypsies found a dead hog lying on the ground near the outdoor market. They carried it to their cave with the intention of eating it. The police retrieved the animal to prevent this from occurring." To verify the account, I talked to the chief of the municipal police who said to me, "I have no recollection of any such incident." My inclination was to accept the police version.

Antonio and Isabel ate with heads low over their food. Antonio ate and drank with zest, spilling wine on the table and on my clothing. When eating olives, he scattered the pits onto the floor as though he were in a city bar, where the clients tossed the bones from fried sardines and the remnants of other *tapas* onto the floor for dogs to devour. Isabel never complained. She swept and mopped at least twice a day.

At that first meal, they gave me a clean cloth napkin that was hanging with several others from a nail driven into the earthen wall, and a knife and fork. But one evening after I had been there several times, Antonio said,

"Let's eat in the Gypsy way."

"*Está bien*," I replied. "How?"

"With our fingers," was Antonio's reply.

He broke off two chunks of bread from the round loaf on the table. Giving one to me, he took the other, and dunked it into a pan of hot tomatoes and peppers that Isabel had just cooked with olive oil. When the bread had soaked up enough juice, he withdrew it and gulped it down. Stray pieces of tomato and pepper he took with his fingers.

I followed his example and we ate together in a kind of ceremonial style while Isabel watched. Isabel's mother and Concha entered the cave and nodded their approval, for to them and to Antonio and Isabel, eating with their fingers was another means of holding onto their Gypsiness. They could do it in the privacy of their cave as a family. "We eat with our fingers, because we want to," said Antonio. "It is the Gypsy way."

At first, I wasn't successful, and Isabel would tactfully place a fork in front of me. Later, if I reached for a fork, she might admonish me, saying, "*No, como un gitano!*" Some foods, like fried fish, were easy to handle, and with practice I became more proficient, so that one night when Isabel gave me a fork by mistake, I protested, saying to her amusement, "Ah, for the *payo*." She knew that I had said *payo* in jest. I might also have used *busne*, a common word for the non-Gypsy in Borrow's day, but almost forgotten now. Another word with the same meaning in other Romany dialects, *gazho* or *gacho*, is rarely used in Guadix.

I hadn't recognized it at the time, but I later realized that, when Antonio gave me the chunk of bread to eat with, it was a further introduction into Gypsy life, not as dramatic as the letting of blood, but equally effective. As a boy, I had wondered how a non-Gypsy was admitted into the Gypsy world. Now, I knew. It was by degrees. With me, the first step was Antonio's invitation to visit his cave. Before the next step, Antonio and Isabel carefully observed how I spoke to the neighbors, how I handled myself with Isabel's mother, and how I got along with the children. After having passed this screening, the invitation came to eat with the family, and finally, the instructions in eating in the Gypsy way. My initiation and the unraveling of the peculiarities of the Gypsies had gone hand in hand. I was learning secrets, which although known by their poor cave-dwelling neighbors, were unknown to the *payos* in the city below and to *payos* elsewhere, for the Gypsies used them to maintain their separation from the non-Gypsy world.

Isabel did not reserve special eating utensils for the use of the *payo*. She had no fear of being contaminated by me, as Gypsies in the United States would have been, and we often ate from a communal plate or pan and drank from the same glasses. The family was free of other fears of contamination, known elsewhere in the Gypsy world as *marime*. It did not bother Antonio when a woman walked over the roof of his cave, as it would an American Gypsy who prefers living quarters with no floors overhead to avoid defilement from women passing over him. And unlike American Gypsies, Antonio and other Guadix male Gypsies had no reservations about urinating in front of other men.

At my first meal in the cave, Isabel did not sit down with Antonio and me at the table where we were eating—she kept busy about the stove. "Perhaps she isn't hungry," I thought, but about a week later, I was again in the cave having supper when a teen-age girl was helping with the children. Only after Antonio and I finished did she and Isabel eat. A few weeks later, though, when we had a meal of snails, Isabel sat down with us, possibly because she considered me to be closer to the family by then. In other Gypsy caves where I ate, the women did not join the men in eating, and I have since found this to be a world-wide Gypsy custom.

One day Antonio appeared to be teaching José to read from a school book. As the boy read, Antonio corrected him if he made a mistake. My reaction was, "How wonderful! Antonio is a model father." I didn't change my opinion a few weeks later when I found out the truth. He had a medical prescription filled, but could not read the directions. After explaining them, I said, "But Antonio, you were helping Joselito with his reading."

"It was all from memory," he replied. "Isabel read the page to me earlier, and I memorized it."

Perhaps Joselito would be one of the handful of Gypsies in Spain who attend school for several years. Unlike most Gypsy parents, who prefer that their children receive only a year or two of education, Antonio and Isabel had other ideas for Joselito. He did well in his first year. This was not surprising, for school teachers had told me that Gypsy children, because of their early freedom, learn much faster than non-Gypsy children.

Joselito took pleasure in correcting my Spanish pronunciation. He would stand next to me, sometimes with children from the neighborhood caves, and, pointing to various parts of my body ask me for their names in Spanish. If I didn't know the word, or if I mispronounced it, he would gleefully set me straight. Antonio was more brusque. If I mispronounced a word, he would look at me sternly and say, "That word doesn't exist!"

Despite their interest in my Spanish, I would have to go elsewhere to enlarge my Caló vocabulary, because the family knew only the most common words such as:

| | | | |
|---|---|---|---|
| *chaboró* | boy | *mutrar* | to urinate |
| *chaborí* | girl | *pañí* | water |
| *churí* | knife | *patu* | father |
| *chuquel* | dog | *payo* | non-Gypsy |
| *matu* | mother | *rom* | Gypsy man and husband |
| *mol* | wine | *romí* | wife |
| *romí* | Gypsy woman | *tapiyar* | to drink |

Antonio, though, taught me a word I hadn't heard. "Do you know what '*nahela!*' means?" he asked. When I said that I didn't, he replied, "It means, 'Get out of here!' so you must be careful how you use it." Later, I learned that it was from the verb *nahelar* (to go), and that I could use it in everyday conversation as, "*Nahelo a mi quer.*" (I am going to my house.)

I used to puzzle over what cave living did to the health of the *cueveros*. Antonio's family was healthy, but what about other cave dwellers? Miguel, the waiter, maintained that caves were healthful. "They have good ventilation from their tall chimneys," he said. Falcó, though, argued that caves brought on cases of arthritis. An article in *El Accitano*, a newspaper published in Guadix in the 1890s, stated that caves were healthful, but today's doctors express no opinions in support of or against caves as housing.

Isabel's health habits should give her children an advantage over non-Gypsy children, if it is true that babies are healthier when their mothers have abstained from alcohol and tobacco. She did not smoke, and drank only lightly, whereas many Castilian women smoked as well as drank.

One day Antonio asked, "Would you like to live in a cave? There is an empty one in good condition not far from mine."

It was a tempting offer. I would have been among the Gypsies all day long, observing their every move, but I declined. I would have had no time to write. The *cueveros* would have visited me night and day. I was also reluctant to antagonize Falcó and other friends in the city below who would not have understood my moving in among cave dwellers, for I relied on them for their knowledge of the city and for their views of life in Guadix.

Frequently when I visited Antonio and Isabel, neighbors were in the cave: Concha, Black Beret, as I called the neighbor who always wore

*Burros and mules are being replaced by tractors and trucks, but they are still used by cave dwellers who cultivate plots of land outside the cave city.*

a beret, or Isabel's mother. The women picked up and kissed the children. The men sat apart and talked, smoked and drank. Children ran in and out of the cave. No one knocked at the door or asked permission to enter. During one of these gatherings, I was drinking wine with Antonio and Black Beret in front of the cave. For several days, the result of a lead from Black Beret, they had been picking peaches, walking two miles to the orchards. We had almost finished one bottle of wine, and I had sent Joselito and Black Beret's little girl, Toiñetta, to the tavern of Ramón de la Toñica to pick up another bottle. Isabel was busy inside the cave, but came out regularly to check on the children. After I offered her some wine, which she declined before returning to the cave, Black Beret said to me,

"You know, Isabel doesn't like wine. She prefers beer, but she has *verguenza* (a sense of shame) and is reluctant to mention it."

I was surprised. Gypsies in Spain are supposed to be *sin verguenza* (without shame), because they fail to follow the moral standards of the majority. They beg, sit on curbstones, are brazen and object to fixed work hours. Yet, here was a Castilian—and although a poor one, familiar with the views of the city's shopkeepers—telling me that Gypsies did have a sense of shame. His comments shocked me into realizing that the label *sin verguenza* was a designation of the merchants, and not used by everyone. To the poor non-Gypsies among whom the Gypsies live, Gypsies are neighbors and people—not outcasts.

Antonio, as well as Isabel, had a sense of shame. Now that we were friends, he was reluctant to accept money after shining my shoes. I had to resort to dropping change into his shoe-shine kit among his brushes and polish. But even this was only partly successful, because he would then insist on leading me by the arm to a nearby bar to buy me a glass of wine.

As I continued to think about what Black Beret had said, it came to me that the moral code of the Gypsies, despite what the store owners might believe, was as strict as theirs. As Falcó had said, prostitution was rare among them. There were no Gypsies among the prostitutes of Guadix. And I remembered that the Caló vocabulary, down to a few hundred words, had four related to morality: *fetel* (good); *chachipé* (truth); *jojana* (lie); *lachi* (shame).

What I had seen of Antonio's family confirmed the poet's statement that the family was the core of Gypsy life, and nothing that I learned later changed my view. It is a myth that Gypsies are sexually promiscuous, or that the men have several wives as the jacket of a record by Sabicas, the Gypsy guitarist, reads. Pity the poor woman whom Antonio might bring home to establish a polygamous household! Isabel would have a knife ready to use on her.

# 6

# The Hokkano Baro

Gypsies seem to have been born
into the world for the sole
purpose of being thieves.

        THE LITTLE GYPSY GIRL (1613)
        *Cervantes*

On one of my early visits to Antonio's cave, an older Gypsy couple entered. He was in his 60s, she in her upper 50s. Each had a deep brown complexion. The woman had a full, robust figure and was wearing an apron over her red skirt. Her coal black hair was pulled straight back, tied with a pink ribbon in the back of her head. Green pendants dangled from her ears. The man was strongly built and had a deeply lined, open face, but could not see well because of running eyes. Antonio introduced them as his parents. They sat down, drank some wine, and had small talk with Antonio and Isabel.

Within a few minutes, the *gitana* began to talk to me. I sensed a change in the atmosphere. At first I didn't understand what she was saying, but eventually I realized from the tone of her soft, sing-song voice and the words I was catching that she was softening me up to ask for money. It was what her ancestors had done in the 1400s on their arrival in Spain. If I had been a woman, I might have heard something like this sixteenth century chant:

| | |
|---|---|
| *Cara de Pazcua florida* | Face of Easter |
| *cara de azuzena y rroza* | Face of lily and rose |

But since I was a man, what I heard was:

You are a grand señor
Life is hard
We are poor
Can you not help us?

I was taken aback. Didn't this violate Gypsy hospitality? Or was it expected of me to give to other members of the family because I had been admitted to the household?

While these thoughts were running through my mind, I had only a few seconds to reach a decision. To gain more time and to get the reaction of Antonio and his wife, I asked, "Antonio, what did she say?" Antonio repeated it in a calm, matter-of-fact voice as if this were an ordinary request.

So I decided to give them something. To have refused would have been more embarrassing than to give. It might also have brought to an end my relationship with Antonio. So I gave the *gitana* a one hundred peseta bill, then worth about two dollars.

I continued to puzzle over this incident, and during the next few weeks, I gradually reconstructed what had happened. Antonio had considered me as a pigeon to be plucked. He could not bring himself to do it, but could see sharing me with his relatives. As I found out later, the older couple — they lived farther up in the cave area — were not his parents. The woman was his aunt, his mother's sister. I learned this from a Castilian friend whose cave I was visiting. The couple passed by his cave, and I mentioned that they were Antonio's parents.

"Not so," said my friend. "They have no children."

And a week after that in a bar near the caves I was introduced to Antonio's real father, a little wizened man with a stubbly beard, smoking the stub of a cigarette, who gave me the impression of being in his cups most of the time.

What Antonio had done was in keeping with an old Gypsy tradition of taking advantage of the *payo*. I could not feel angry. Nor could I be upset about the old couple. The husband seemed to be in poor health and no doubt needed money. Furthermore, I was a new experience in Antonio's life, as he was in mine. I asked myself how else a poor Gypsy bookblack, who had, no doubt, heard how easy it was to get money from foreign tourists, should react to having a target of opportunity like myself in his cave home, an apparently wealthy *payo* who drove an automobile and lived in the hotel. Nonetheless, I admit to having been disillusioned, because once in Antonio's home I had assumed that I could relax and not worry about being imposed upon.

My disillusionment, though, was not as severe as Walter Starkie's. In *Raggle Taggle* he described a disenchanting experience he had in Rumania after World War I. Remembering George Borrow's description of the value attached by the Spanish Gypsies to the modesty of their women, he was not prepared when a Gypsy woman offered her favors to him. "Alas O Borrow!" he exclaimed, "Where are your theories about the chastity of Gypsy women?"

Borrow's views are still valid in Spain, but there are exceptions. In Seville in the Alameda de Hércules park, famous in the last century for the flamenco bars which surrounded it, but now run-down and a sleeping place for drunks, I spoke with a middle-aged Gypsy prostitute sitting on a bench waiting for clients. What first attracted my attention to her was that she was alone. In Spain a Gypsy woman rarely leaves her dwelling unless she has a child with her, other *gitanas* or her husband. Also in Seville, a Gypsy antique dealer in back of the cathedral offered for a fee to provide me with a Gypsy girl for the evening.

I had Starkie in mind when I visited Lorca, an ancient city in Murcia province. In *In Sara's Tents*, he had referred to both the city and its Gypsies as being aristocratic. The old plaza, surrounded with baroque buildings, was every bit as lovely as he had described it. I then went looking for the Gypsies. I found them while driving along the narrow road below the great castle which stands above the city when I was forced to stop to avoid piles of human excrement and broken glass spread across the road. From the mouth of a cave alongside the road five dirty, naked children of both sexes, followed by a mother with a baby in her arms, charged toward me—all begging. I had been ambushed! I said to myself while deciding how much to give them, "Alas O Starkie: where are your aristocratic Gypsies of Lorca?"

The older couple's act in Antonio's cave was not in the same class with what Borrow called the *hokkano baro*, or great trick, practiced by the Gypsies through the ages. Borrow described how a *gitana* swindled a Castilian woman in the 1830s by persuading her to deposit her jewelry in a designated location on the belief that it would multiply. The Gypsy then replaced it with false jewelry and absconded with the genuine jewelry. A Gypsy hoax is also described by Jerónimo de Alcalá in 1624 in his *Alonzo de Muchos Amos* in which a widow is swindled of her jewels on the pretext that she will acquire a great treasure. Starkie tells how a victim bought from a Gypsy a "money-making" machine which supposedly transformed raw metal into coins.

The greatest trick of the Gypsies in their over five hundred years in Western Europe is the fable of their origin, a fable which they successfully foisted onto credulous societies unprepared for this swordless invasion of colorful wanderers from the East. On their arrival they said they were penitents forced to leave Egypt because they had refused to receive the Holy Family when it fled there from the Holy Land. (From the word Egypt has come English *Gypsy*, French *gitan* and Spanish *gitano*.) Another tale was that they had forged the nails used in the Crucifixion and had been wandering ever since to atone for this sin.

So under the guise of being penitents, they were accepted by European rulers and even by Pope Martin V, who accepted the various titles that the chiefs used: Dukes and Counts of Little or Lower Egypt. This acceptance lasted in any given country for about fifty years until the novelty wore off. They were then seen, according to the German scholar H.M. Grellman in the eighteenth century, to be the "mere refuse of humanity."

I find it amusing today, several hundred years later, that the Gypsies of Guadix, and many other Gypsies, have been tricked by their own deception. The few who have thought much about their origin believe it to be Egypt. India, the homeland, has been forgotten.

Gypsies in Guadix, though, no longer try to perform the great trick. When I told the chief of police in Guadix how Gypsy palmists in the United States swindle non-Gypsies of large sums of money, he commented, "That sort of thing does not occur here."

I have used Borrow's term, *hokkano baro*, for the swindles and tricks of the Gypsies, because he has made the expression known to English readers, but in Caló it is known as *jojana bara*. (*Jojana* comes from the Sanskrit *kuhana* (lie) and *bara* from *vadra* (big).) The *jojana bara* that I experienced in Antonio's cave was more of a trick than a swindle, a trick to make the couple's begging easier. Begging is a centuries' old Gypsy custom, and the Guadix Gypsies haven't forgotten it. They still have their own word in Caló for it, *mangar*.

As I had found earlier, any stranger is a target for begging by Gypsy and non-Gypsy children. They may ask for cigarettes, but usually beg for money. "*Un duro! Un duro!*" In fairness to them, it is the foreign visitors who are partly to blame. For years they have given money to Gypsies to pose for photos. A natural second step is for the Gypsies to offer themselves to the tourist to have their picture taken for a fee, and finally, to ask for money whether the tourist has a camera or not.

Among the caves above the city of Baza I had an experience which showed how Gypsies, once accustomed to it, continue with begging. I was walking with some friends from the city below. "Our Gypsies do not beg," they said. I had no reason to doubt their statement for the caves are not visible from the Murcia-Granada highway, and tourists do not visit them. As we strolled along chatting with a Gypsy family here and a Castilian family there, we experienced no begging until surrounded by a band of naked Gypsy children who ran down to us from a poorly maintained cave.

"*Pesetas!* Money!" they shouted, using "peseta" and "money" interchangeably.

They had only recently returned with their parents from Alicante, a coast resort, where the children begged from tourists and had learned the English word for money. A school teacher in our group gave them a few pesetas, but admonished them for begging from strangers.

As I moved about Spain and begging Gypsies approached me, I would sometimes say, "*Chaborós*, a Gypsy child doesn't beg from strangers." But this didn't make much sense to a Gypsy child whose parents had probably encouraged him to beg. At least, it took the children by surprise to be addressed as *chaboró*, and they scurried away. A more effective response was, "*No tengo jayeres*," (I don't have any money) using *jayeres*, a Caló word for money. I might also say, "*Me duele el pecho*," which is slang for having no money. In Iznalloz, when three healthy-looking Gypsy children approached me asking for money, I felt of their full stomachs. "You don't look hungry to me." They found this amusing and laughed with me.

But I sometimes gave a few coins to children both in Guadix and in other parts of Spain. (I also sent money to Antonio and his family at Christmas.) This gave me a closer look at strange Gypsies than I otherwise would have had.

I remember an incident in front of the old church on the main street of Antequerra, a lovely city to the west of Granada. My wife had been in the church while I remained outside. I had given a coin to a *gitana* who was begging in front of the church with a baby in her arms—Castilian women entering and leaving the church also gave her coins. When my wife left the church she, too, made a contribution just before I joined her. I said in jest to the Gypsy, "You have succeeded with both of us." She saw the humor of the situation and acknowledged with a light, soft smile that this was so.

"Beggars in Guadix," Falcó had once told me, "were common twenty years ago, but are rarely seen today." He was right, but during the early years of my visits, two old Gypsy women, each wearing the petticoats of a by-gone era, slowly walked along the streets begging in voices so soft that I could hardly hear them. An old Castilian woman also begged, and when the two Gypsies died in the late 1970s, she was the only woman beggar left. She made the rounds of all the shops but since she rarely bathed, Falcó and the store owners forbade her to enter their shops. She patiently waited outside until receiving money from them. About this time an old man, a non-Gypsy, began to beg. This so surprised the Gypsies that they said in Caló, "*Endica el payo!*" (Look at the *payo!*) Castilians overhearing them picked up the expression and began to use it themselves. So the last two beggars in the city were not Gypsies, but *payos*.

As I have already mentioned, I held no grudge against Antonio for the incident of the *hokkano baro*, and continued to visit him and his family in their cave. I also decided it was best to adopt the same attitude toward the fictitious parents, Rodrigo and Rosario. I saw them frequently in the city where he was a bootblack and lottery vendor. Two or three times a week, I bought lottery tickets from them. I would also buy them an occasional glass of wine in one of the bars when they entered seeking clients. We became friendly and, although restricted to brief conversations we had on the street and in various bars, we found out a lot about each other. Rodrigo wore shirts with long sleeves, which he rolled up in the hot summer months, exposing a series of tatoos dating from his service as a young man in the Navy after enlisting in his home town of Málaga. He came to Guadix after his Navy duty when he married Rosario, and had lived high up in the cave area ever since.

In their youth, he and Rosario must have been a handsome couple. They still had good features and strong physiques, and were always well dressed. "When Rodrigo was a young man in the 1930s," said Falcó, "he was noted for the large size of his male appendage. Castilian women went out of their way to catch a glimpse of its outline when he sat on his stool shining shoes."

Disaster struck Rosario and Rodrigo in the third year of our relationship. "Rodrigo has gone blind," Antonio told me. "It was an eye disease. Don't you remember how his eyes were inflamed and running? Well, they got worse. Now he can't see. He has to wear black glasses, use a white-tipped cane, and be led by his wife who alerts him to who is coming so he can greet them."

I admired the courage with which they faced their misfortune. They made up their minds to carry on as before. They were still neatly dressed, she in her bright, Gypsy colors and he in his clean white shirts. In cool weather he wore a jacket and green hat with a feather in it. He had to stop shining shoes, but with his wife continued to sell lottery tickets. They came down the street from the caves an hour later than before, arriving at nine in the morning. In visiting the bars in search of clients, they had their usual *café con leche* or a glass of wine. One day, when I was chatting with them on the sidewalk in front of the Banco Nacional, a Gypsy boy was pestering me to shine my shoes. Rodrigo told the boy to leave, and, nodding his head toward me, said *"Chaboró, es de la familia."* (Boy, he is of the family.) Among Gypsies, *"de la familia"* means that the person referred to is a Gypsy. But obviously I was not a Gypsy, which is why the boy looked back over his shoulder in a perplexed manner as he left us.

Another time, Rosario, having rebuked a *gitana* who was begging from me, gave a further reason why I should not have been bothered. *"Es compadre de Antonio."* She introduced me to her sister from Granada, who had a clothing stand at the Saturday market, as *"Un amigo de lo gitano."*

# 7

# The Cave Tavern
# of Ramón de la Toñica

We came to a cave which was more like
a robber's den than a tavern. A
gloomy smoky hole it was…thronged
with dishevelled Gypsies.

DON GYPSY (1936)
*Walter Starkie*


Antonio not only introduced me to his home and family, but he opened another door onto Gypsy life and that of the other *cueveros* by introducing me to the cave tavern of Ramón de la Toñica. The men of the cave city thought of it as their club. My introduction to it came one evening when Antonio, tired from a hot August day of dashing through the streets seeking clients, was sitting on the battered box containing his shoe-shine gear in front of the Bar Dólar. *"Hola!"* I said, "Do you want a beer?"

"Let's go up to the tavern of Ramón," he said.

"That suits me fine," I replied, and Antonio directed me to the lower reaches of the cave city, not far from where we had walked together on my first visit to the caves with him. Caves now alternated with houses. Miguel the waiter lived in one of the last houses. Just after passing it, I stopped the car to wait for a herd of fifty goats to pass in front of us.

Thirty yards higher, up a steep open slope, Antonio had me pull up alongside a high, windowless, white-washed cave front gleaming in the early evening sunlight. The only indication of its being a drinking place was a small beer sign. It looked like the residential cave it had been before it was transformed into a tavern about one hundred years ago. The only clues to the activity which went on inside were the six or

60

seven men out front playing a horse-shoe like game associated with bars and taverns, and five or six clients sitting with their chairs against the face of the cave, some drinking, others just basking in the sun.

Walking past the clients, we arrived at the tavern's only entrance. Antonio, leading the way, pushed aside the cloth hanging over the doorway, and descended the two steps leading down into the cave. We were in a room about twenty by twenty feet square. It had a tile floor and walls of two colors, beige from the floor about half-way up, and then a dull blue. A light bulb without a globe dangled from the ceiling. An old bull-fight print behind the bar was flanked with two copper plates. An image of the Virgin was on one wall. Near the entrance were two old paintings, one of the cave and one of the Arab fortress below.

Several clients, Gypsy and Castilian, were sitting on small cane stools, leaning against the walls and quietly talking. Directly in front of us was a wooden bar about ten feet long. Behind it stood the bartender-owner. A tall, strong-looking Castilian about sixty, he was wearing a reddish-brown sweater and a dark blue beret.

Antonio walked up to him saying, *"Buenas tardes Pepe,"* and ordered a half liter of wine—which cost fifteen cents. Pepe filled an earthenware pitcher from a cask of wine from La Mancha, by reputation the best wine in Guadix.

Pepe del Ramón didn't look like any bartender I had ever known. On his morning walk into the city of houses with his conservative suit coat and sober, stately demeanor, he looked more like the director of a funeral home than a bartender. Most tavern owners were outgoing and welcomed customers, but not Pepe. He did not discourage business, but his bored expression did nothing to help it along. On rare occasions a half smile showed on his face, but he never laughed outright.

His belief was that the location of the tavern filled a need for the *cueveros*, so barring unexpected developments it would always have clients who needed no special encouragement from him except to be there while he tapped the casks from La Mancha. There were other taverns in the city of caves, but none was as popular as his. Once in the city below when I asked Pepe how business was, he replied, "Always the same. It's the same, because my clients drink the same amount every night." This meant that Pepe could plan his buying accurately and, with a low overhead, could count on a profit.

One spring when Pepe and his wife went to Madrid to attend the communion of a grandson, they closed the tavern for a long weekend. The clients were upset. For three days they had to fend for themselves, passing their time in other drinking places while waiting for the tavern to reopen. The closing became the principal subject of conversation among the dwellers of the cave city. Wherever I went, Gypsies and poor Castilians said to me with concern, "Ramón is closed."

Like bartenders everywhere, clients often used Pepe to settle minor disputes. His ability to read was an asset—many of his clients could not read well enough to understand articles in the press—and an argument-clinching statement was, "Pepe read it."

His estimation of me rose when he saw me one day in the Bar Dólar having a cup of coffee with a highly respected teacher from the local academy. A few days later, he opened a discussion with me in the tavern. "Have you seen this article?" he asked, pointing to a piece he was reading in the Granada newspaper about an Argentinian boxer who had died in a house of prostitution in Reno, Nevada. As we talked about it, my stature grew in the eyes of the clients.

When Antonio returned with the wine and two glasses—there was no waiter—he set them on top of a full cask of wine standing in one corner. The tops of the casks were also useful as table tops for setting out snacks. I liked them because they made good leaning posts. Alongside us, a half liter of wine with an empty glass next to it stood on top of a cask. I wondered to whom it belonged. I soon found out. A blind Gypsy of about sixty came down the steps into the cave and walked to the cask. The wine must be his, I thought. "May I fill your glass?" I asked. After I filled it, he thanked me, gulped it down, and went outside to join his cronies. We repeated the procedure several more times that evening.

Antonio nodded to a Castilian who was reading a newspaper at the end of the bar while leaning against the keg from which Pepe was drawing wine. "*Se llama* Ambrosio," said Antonio. He had a small, neatly clipped mustache and wore a brown cap. Antonio told me that he was a construction worker and was known for his skill in snaring birds at their drinking places in the early morning hours. His cave, which he later invited me to visit after we had become friends from drinking together, was near the tavern. It was a comfortable dwelling with wallpaper in the rooms. In the cave yard was a well, thirty-five feet deep, a shade tree and a flower and vegetable garden.

I used to tease him about his reserved position at the cask—he was there every night. I would borrow his newspaper, and assuming his

An early morning view of the cave tavern of Ramón de la Toñica, the
most popular of the bars in the city of caves.

Pepe always wears a suit
and tie for his morning
stroll in the city below.
Beside him is Ambrosio,
one of his regular
clients.

stance, say to him, "It's my turn." One evening when I entered the cave, another client was leaning on the keg reading the newspaper. Pretending to be disturbed, I said, "You have Ambrosio's place." He gravely left the keg and returned the paper to Ambrosio. This caused even solemn Pepe to give one of his half smiles.

I asked Antonio how many rooms there were in the tavern. I had already seen one directly in back of the bar, a sort of store room, and I could see the entrances to two others.

"Seven," said Antonio. "Come along. I'll show you."

I followed him, carrying our pitcher of wine. We passed through the archway on our left into a television room, large enough to hold fifteen viewers easily. Seven or eight clients were watching an American western on a black and white television which had better reception than the one in the hotel, probably because there was less interference in the cave city than in the city below. Next was a card room. "They play for drinks, not money," said Antonio. Of the five players sitting at the table, three were Gypsies and two were Castilians. I hadn't anticipated this intermingling of Gypsies and non-Gypsies. There was nothing in the books I had read in the Library of Congress about Gypsies drinking and playing cards nightly with non-Gypsies.

There was yet another room beyond, used only by Pepe and his wife when they wanted to enter their residential cave above without going outdoors. They did so by climbing a steep stairway, cut into the natural earth, which wound in darkness from the lower level to a bedroom in the upper cave.

As we stood in the card room watching the game and sipping our wine, I thought about the description of the tavern that Walter Starkie had written in *Don Gypsy* fifty years ago: "A gloomy smoky hole it was..." Pepe's tavern with its smoke-filled, underground rooms and its dim lighting did seem a likely hangout of Gypsy thieves, and the clients with their dark faces, black hair and wild-looking expressions looked the part of robbers. But my first visit was long enough to note that there were as many non-Gypsy patrons as Gypsies. And with Antonio's introduction, the features of this wild-appearing people seemed to soften. And, later, when I became on good terms with them, I learned that they were far from being robbers. They were Castilian laborers and Gypsy bootblacks and lottery vendors wearing their day-to-day clothing of caps, sweaters and coats, passing the evening hours watching television and playing cards before returning home for dinner.

Little had changed in their appearance since Starkie's visit, but what had changed was their geographic horizon. Their world-view had expanded in the past twenty years as a result of having worked in other parts of Spain and Germany, Switzerland and France. Many spoke a few words of foreign languages. With one Gypsy who had worked in a French-speaking canton in Switzerland I used to exchange *"Bonsoir"* and *"Comment ça va?"* And most could say, *"Guten morgen."*

From the deportment of its patrons, the tavern was as much a gentlemen's club as the lyceum of the businessmen in the city below. There was no loud talking, no singing and no rough-housing — Pepe did not permit it. No one seemed to be drinking heavily, and I never saw anyone drunk except one Sunday afternoon a man was lying in the hot sun alongside the tavern sleeping off a night of drinking. Since he was lying on his stomach, I couldn't tell if he were a Gypsy or a Castilian.

Antonio told me a story to illustrate Pepe's ability to maintain order. "A few years ago," he said, "a Gypsy from another part of Spain entered the tavern with some relatives from Guadix who had cautioned him to behave himself—he had a repuation for being a trouble maker. He was quiet while drinking his first few glasses of wine, but after awhile he challenged Pepe by throwing the wine in his glass onto the floor in front of the bar, and then asking for another. Pepe calmly looked at him and said, *'No hay má vino.'* (There is no more wine.) And before the Gypsy could reach for his knife, Pepe levelled a pistol at him. The Gypsy fled from the tavern."

I am certain that Pepe would not permit his clients to use drugs. The police would never have to raid his establishment as they did a tiny bar I visited in Jerez de la Frontera — the home of Sherry wine — in back of the Plaza de Santiago in the old quarter. I had gone there to find out how much Caló the Gypsies knew (it was very little), and to dream about the last century when Jerez was one of the birth places of flamenco. A long-haired, robust Gypsy in his thirties had been singing at the top of his voice, vigorously banging out his accompaniment on top of the bar with his fists. Four youthful non-Gypsies next to him clapped their hands and took turns dancing. After a few minutes, one of them said, *"Cuidado! la policía!"*

Not knowing why the police would have an interest in the bar, I asked, "But can't we talk and sing?"

"Of course," was the reply. "Spain is a democracy."

But it wasn't talking or singing that the police were interested in.

It was drugs. So when a plain clothesman arrived a few moments later, he backed my companions against the wall and searched them. To deter their flight, two uniformed police, armed with sub-machine guns, stood outside the door. Enough evidence was found to warrant their being taken away.

On my next few visits to the tavern of Ramón, I came with Antonio. I was indebted to him for having introduced me to the tavern, but I felt I should eventually go by myself, and I finally worked up the courage to do so. On nervously arriving in front of the tavern, I was reassured when two or three of the habitués nodded toward me, and before I got to the entrance one elderly Castilian offered me something to eat. I didn't know what it was—and I still don't—but I accepted it and ate it. In the tavern or elsewhere, I never declined food or drinks offered to me whether it was a cup of wine or a slice of cucumber. Occasionally, I had an upset stomach, and once I had a twenty-four hour fever.

While munching on the food I saw Miguel the waiter sitting at a table. He motioned for me to join him, and when I did he bought me a glass of wine. From that night on, I felt no inhibitions about visiting the tavern alone. I began to feel at home. I was embarrassed, though, one night when on my arrival several Gypsies kow-towed to me. "*Qué pasa?*" I asked. I had a suspicion what had happened. There are no secrets in Guadix, and the word had reached the cave city that I was a retired colonel—I had told Falcó and a few others. They were playfully letting me know that they knew about it.

Among my drinking companions was Manuel, a tall, dark Gypsy in his 70s. With his even features, prominent nose and black eyes, he would satisfy the most critical Hollywood casting director in search of a movie Gypsy. But there was something about his appearance that separated him from the others. Falcó had also noted this difference.

"When he and his wife come into my shop," he said, "he is more considerate of her than most Gypsies are toward their wives." And I had noticed that he was always neatly dressed, whereas the Guadix Gypsies prided themselves on their careless attire. On a cool spring evening when he was nattily dressed in a brown cap, tan trousers and purple shirt under a sport coat, I asked him where he was from.

"For most of my life," he said, "I lived in Seville where my wife and I sold embroidery. But a few years ago, after my son married a *gitana* from Guadix, my wife and I moved here to be close to them."

"We must be different," he continued, "because other people have asked us the same question. Perhaps, [and this he said in a low voice] we are less savage than the Gypsies here."

A regular client I came to know well was Carlos, an even-tempered Gypsy whose strong physique was admirably suited for his profession; he was a smith, and had his forge in a cave.

Another drinking companion was a Castilian in his 40s, known as Pedro el Moro, because he had worked ten years in the Spanish Sahara and spoke Arabic, and probably because of his dark skin — he was darker than many Gypsies. A big man with strong features, he was as savage looking as any of the card players he joined nightly in the card room. These included el Cebollo (the onion), a dark volatile Castilian, and el Greco, a quiet, self-assured Gypsy. Pedro was a warm, friendly person with a wife and two children. He knew Caló from his long association with the Gypsies — more than Carlos and more than Antonio the bootblack. He grew up with Gypsies in the cave area and still lived there. Once he volunteered, "I like Gypsies. I played with them as a boy. They are my friends." This was an unusual statement to a foreigner who supposedly had the same attitude toward the Gypsies as the store owners.

*Drinking companions at the tavern of Ramón l. to r. Pedro el Moro, Carlos the smith, the author, Torcuato and Pepe el pando.*

He would repeat Caló words that he remembered to see if I knew them. He was proud of his knowledge of languages, and one June evening, feeling the effect of the alcohol he had been drinking at the fiesta of Fátima at the Ermita Novísima on the edge of the cave city, he addressed me in four languages: throaty Arabic, Caló, Spanish and Italian. That night, dressed in a well-fitted suit, he seemed to be a prosperous businessman rather than a poor laborer in a small factory.

Another non-Gypsy card player was Torcuato, who always wore a brown cap when playing. He had only a short distance to travel for his nightly entertainment, because his cave was on the slope just above the tavern. He made his living delivering goods for the merchants to outlying villages on his motorcycle. Like Pedro, he also knew Caló. One evening between card hands he asked, "Do you know what *la de pero* means?"

When I said that I didn't, he poked his stomach with the fingers of one hand. "It means 'knife thrust to the belly.' "

One evening, wishing to confirm the three words I had in Caló for making love, I asked him which ones he knew. "*Querar* and *bandar*," he said, adding, *bandar* also means 'to marry.' "

"Don't forget *rilar*," said Pedro.

These were the words I already had. *Rilar* was a strange one, because it originally meant "to break wind."

Pepe el Gordo, the fat one, also known as Pepe el Pando, a Castilian in his fifties, was one of the tavern's most faithful clients. He never missed a night—unless there was a death or other emergency in the family. Arriving promptly at 7:45, he stayed until 11:30 when he returned home for a light supper before going to bed. Despite his nickname, he wasn't fat, but rather short and sturdy like his Celto-Iberian ancestors.

He and his wife operated a fruit-vegetable stand in the Plaza de Abastos. She had managed it for ten years while as an emigrant worker in Corsica he had saved enough money to buy a comfortable house not far from the tavern. Frequently he would prevent my buying drinks by alerting the bartender not to accept my money. When I would try to pay, I would be told, "paid."

He brought along pieces of cheese, slices of spicy sausage and other tidbits which he shared with me and Carlos, the Gypsy smith. One evening he had a bag of peaches that he cut up and put in a chilled pitcher of wine to make a delicious sangría. He brought food because Pepe de Ramón served no *tapas* to nibble on. "In Guadix," Pepe el

Pando explained, "taverns serve no food. Only bars do, sometimes only *tapas*, but sometimes sandwiches and hot food like pork and french fried potatoes."

A man of few words, Pepe could communicate through facial expressions. One evening a Gypsy was telling me that he had worked in Switzerland. Pepe had only to raise his eyebrows to signal me this was not so. Another evening he chided a youthful Gypsy he felt was speaking to me discourteously.

That first night in the tavern a small, dark Gypsy in his forties with a simian-like face joined Antonio and me. "Do you need a guide, sir?" he asked in English. His accent was good, but when I spoke to him, I found that he knew only a few set phrases such as, "I will show you the caves of the Gypsies." He was another Antonio, also known as *el follare* (the love maker), and was one of the two Gypsy guides who sought out tourists on the highway to guide through the cave city. He was so well-liked throughout Guadix by both Gypsies and Castilians that when I knew him better, I told him in jest that he should run for mayor.

He was witty and enjoyed acting out little skits. One year when I was leaving Guadix, he came to say goodbye. Not content with a simple farewell, he assumed the role of a begging Gypsy, and in a soft, whiny voice said, "Sir, something for the children." A master of the Spanish *piropos* (compliments to passing girls), he would call out on the city streets, "How pretty are the girls of Spain! Most Holy Mary, what a pretty girl!" Referring to me, he might ask, "Would you not like to learn English from a handsome *americano?*" At first, I was embarrassed, but I noticed that the girls never objected to his flattery.

The other guide, Castaño, so called because of his chestnut colored skin, was also present that night in the tavern. He had the innate arrogance and body movements that Hemingway noted among Gypsy bullfighters, and as Theophile Gautier in 1840 observed in his *Voyage in Spain*, a majestic carriage as though conscious of the antiquity of his race.

Meetings with him were not relaxed like the ones with Antonio. His mind was as quick as his darting eyes, and he used it to outwit the person to whom he was talking. He considered himself to be the most Gypsy of all the Gypsies in Guadix. "My name, Heredia," he said, "is more authentic than any other Gypsy name."

He also spoke to me of the superiority of the Gypsies over Castilians. Using *Calé*, the Gypsies' own word for themselves, he said, "*Lo calé son má listo que lo castellano y má elegante.*" (Gypsies are more clever and elegant than Castilians.) He added, "I am too proud of my race to have ever considered marriage to a non-Gypsy." A handsome man, many Castilian women would have willingly married him.

City people now avoided him. He was quick to use his knife, and had been arrested for stabbing the driver of an automobile that struck his motorcycle.

Other Gypsies had let me know of their feeling of superiority. Isabel and her mother had exclaimed, "*Chachipé!*" when I said their children were healthier than children of the city below. But none had stated it as strongly as Castaño. I was learning that this feeling of superiority was at the core of their Gypsiness.

Castaño knew more Caló than any other Gypsy in the city. He had learned it from his father—"My how I loved that man"—who had been a *marchante*. He guarded his knowledge, for he saw Caló as helping the Gypsies to remain apart from the Castilians. At first, it bothered him that I was learning the language, and he used it with me only because I gave him examples of words I had acquired from other Gypsies. He could construct sentences such as the following almost entirely in the language—a rare skill in Spain:

> *Tú y mangue nahar a chorar besti a un paluno.*
> You and I will go to steal animals at a farm
> *Me chapiquelo que abilleya la jundunaré.*
> I'm leaving because the police are coming.

When I last saw him, he was going to work in Switzerland on construction. I wished him good luck, "*Cuando nahela, busca jailleres, jala balichón, tapiya mol y chora algunos churos y jeles en un paluno.*" (When you go, find money, eat meat, drink wine, and steal some mules and burros at a ranch.)

Knowing Castaño, whose father had been a horse trader, helped me to discover the social hierarchy among the Gypsies. It did not depend on personal possessions but on occupation. The Gypsies with the most prestige were the horse traders. Just below them were the smiths—antique dealers of the large cities would also be at this level. Next came the lottery vendors, and well below them market workers and shoe-shiners. I could identify Gypsies in each of these occupations, the horse traders by their distinctive dress and walk, the smiths by their erect carriage, and the bootblacks by their unkempt appearance. Would Lorca have considered them all as making up the most aristo-

(above) The self-assured look of this horse trader reflects his social position, the most prestigious among the Spanish Gypsies.

(left) These bright youths are enjoying the prosperity of the family's antique shop.

cratic element in Spain? I believe he would, which means that Antonio the bootblack, despite his olive skin and un-Gypsy like appearance would be among them along with the horsetraders and smiths because of his pride in being a Gypsy.

Another of the card players, although not a regular, was a ruffianly looking Gypsy of eighteen, the model of the wild, primitive Gypsy that my friends in Granada had told me to expect in the caves of Guadix. Bushy eyebrows and a thick nose with wide nostrils were set in an almost black face. Unruly, long, black hair tumbled to his neck. His shirt was unbuttoned to the waist and he wore a narrow, beaded necklace. But despite his ferocious appearance, he had an amiable personality — at least when among his friends.

I first met him on the road to Benalúa when I gave him a lift in my car. Later, when descending a dusty trail in the city of caves I heard a voice call out, *"Ay gitano!"* It was *"el negrito,"* as I called him in my notes — his name was "Angel" — with a teenage girl and two small children. "This is my wife of five years," he said. "I was thirteen and she was fourteen when we married."

His wife, a pretty girl with a brown skin, stood demurely at his side. She appeared to be much in love with him, and he with her. They were leaving for Alicante to pick tomatoes where they could earn more money than in Guadix.

The humor in the tavern was simple and if an amusing incident could be easily retold, it was related indefinitely. One evening I was nibbling on some small, hot peppers with Carlos the smith and Pepe el Pando. Carlos, who had swallowed a piece of the white, hot center, shouted,

*"Pica! Pica!"* (It stings! It stings!)

(No matter that he had been eating peppers daily for over fifty years and should not have been surprised.)

*"Pica?"* asked Pepe in feigned surprise. Then, answering his own question, he said, *"No pica."*

*"Sí, pica!"* responded Carlos.

Pepe calmly shook his head and continued to munch on his pepper.

I then got into the act with a few of my own *"picas."*

Whatever the humorous merits of the incident, it went on with variations for several more minutes, and was repeated on future evenings that year, and in the years that followed. I even heard it from members of the families of the two men.

Another story, told year after year, was Pepe el Pando's account of my giving him and his wife a ride home on a rainy day after they had finished work in the market. When I had seen them passing by the hotel, just as I was about to get into my car, I had considered it only natural to offer them a ride, but in their eyes it was highly unusual, because *señoritos* of the city do not pick up market workers in their automobiles. Another subject of conversation was my trips. "How long did it take you to get here?" "How far away is America?" "How much do you pay to rent the car?"

Despite the intermingling of Gypsies and Castilians in the tavern, there was one area, the cave room to the right of the bar room, reserved, apparently by mutual consent, for the use of Castilians for card playing. I never saw any Gypsies in it. Discrimination in the cave tavern of Ramón de la Toñica? Yes, I suppose it can be called that, but the Gypsies had their turn. Sunday afternoons — again by mutual consent — was reserved for them. On these afternoons, the tavern was full of Gypsies, inside and outside — and no Castilians. Gypsy wives stood out front on the stone floor of an old *era* talking in groups while their children played. And there were even a few *gitanas* inside with their husbands, something that rarely happened during the week, because then the tavern was for men. The Gypsy hour lasted from early afternoon until six or seven o'clock when the *gitanas* returned to their homes and the usual Castilian clients arrived to mix with the Gypsies already there.

One evening, while sitting near the door with Pepe el Pando watching a heavy rain falling outside the cave, I noticed the small figure of a *gitana* of an undetermined age, with the blackest face I had ever seen on a Gypsy, sitting on a stool in the television room. She was holding a baby in her arms and her figure was smothered in layers of clothing. Her face was almost hidden by several scarves tied around her head. She was sitting near her husband, a full-bearded Gypsy, who had once politely invited me to have a drink with him.

"Are they from Guadix?" I asked Pepe.

"No. He is from Alicante, but has lived here for about fifteen years. She comes from Huescar, beyond Baza."

Women seldom entered the tavern, but on this stormy night she was waiting for her husband to finish his drink and to help her home with a heavy sack of vegetables. "Are you ready to go?" she asked him.

"Not yet. You go," he replied, continuing a lively discussion with his friends.

She then left the bar, going out into the rain with the sack of vegetables under one arm and the baby under the other.

In about half an hour, she returned. As she glided past my seat at the cave entrance, I saw that her outer layer of clothing and the baby's were soaking wet. She stood with her back to the bar, tears running down her face—but not saying a word. In a few minutes her husband left and she followed him. I never knew whether she did not have the key to their cave, or whether she simply wanted her husband to come home. It could have been the latter, because when I told Falcó about it, he said, "My wife and I have seen that Gypsy beat his wife whom we call *la negra gitana*. She loved him deeply, and, beatings or not, was always with him, a few steps behind, or seeking him out in the bars and taverns of the city."

Several months later, however, she had no husband to beat her. During a dispute near their family cave, another Gypsy stabbed him to death. Antonio showed me the spot, close to his cave, with blotches of blood still on the ground. This reminded me again that the soft-spoken Gypsies with whom I was drinking were the same Gypsies known throughout Spain for their fierceness and readiness to resort to violence. As with the death of the Benalúa Gypsy in the city below, the reasons for the conflict were not clear. El Cebollo told me that it was because the husband had made eyes at another *gitano's* wife. If that were so, death had come at the hands of a jealous husband avenging the slighted honor of his wife.

Could it be, I wondered, that the reason for the Gypsies' sporadic bloodletting was that they had held onto the concept of honor of Spain of the 1600s longer than the other residents of Iberia? During that era, the Golden Age of Spanish literature, playwrights based their plays on affairs of honor, but time had eroded this idea of high honor. The Gypsies' clinging to it would confirm what the poet in Falcó's shop had said about the Gypsies being more Spanish than the Spanish themselves.

My acceptance by both Gypsies and non-Gypsies in the tavern meant that I had succeeded in crossing the cultural abyss that separated them from me. In doing so, I had established a warm relationship with the cave dwellers. I wasn't sure how I had done this, because from the start I had realized that I was conspicuous. I felt that my approach must be a natural and honest one in which I showed my interest in them, in their daily lives and in their families.

The only time I ever told a lie in Spain was to some Gypsies in a bar in Jaén province. To speed up getting acquainted with them, a devil of some kind within me prompted me to tell them that my grandmother was a Gypsy, a fiction they readily accepted, because of my knowledge of Caló. As one of them expressed it, "How else would a foreign *payo* learn Caló except through a relative with *aratí?*" I always regretted the incident. (*Aratí* means blood in Caló, but as used here it refers to Gypsy blood.)

The hospitality of the *cueveros* was extended quietly. Few of them could afford to offer me a half liter of wine as did Pepe el Pando, so they made me feel at home with a nod, a brief smile, or by making room for me to sit down. I learned that it was possible to sit among them and yet feel close to them without carrying on a conversation, because they often went minutes at a time without talking. This was unexpected, because most Spanish in public places are extremely talkative.

I had good reason to worry about not being accepted, because on that first visit with Antonio, I noticed there were no clients from the city below. Later, Falcó, who had come to accept my going among the Gypsies, said to me, "I would never consider going into the tavern. I would be uncomfortable." A university student who went with me once was ill at ease. Aside from the face-to-face reaction of the clients to my presence, I received a report from another source. María, the Castilian cook in the hotel, and, herself a cave dweller, said to me, "They say," nodding her head in approval, "there is a tall foreigner who speaks Castilian (the Spanish language), and drinks and talks with everyone in the tavern of Ramón de la Toñica."

For my part, I found that I liked being with the tavern's clients, Gypsies and non-Gypsies, as I had enjoyed meeting the cave-boys who had swooped down upon me some weeks before. I asked myself why I felt this way. Was it the dignified manner in which they carried themselves despite their poverty? Was it their acceptance of one another's racial differences? Or was it because their approval of me, a stranger, was flattering to my vanity? Whatever the reason, I agreed with Borrow to whom the "lower class" were an extraordinary people, proud and independent, a people to admire.

I didn't think of them as a class, though, but as individuals: Torcuato with a twinkle in his eye, sober Pedro el Moro and cool-faced Pepe el Pando. Borrow was referring to non-Gypsies, but I included Gypsies as well, for the two groups had much in common after centuries of sharing the same land. If Manuel Azaña, President of the Second Republic, was correct in stating that the national roots of Spain are preserved in their purest form among the poor, then despite the disapproval of my merchant friends in the city below, I was in good company.

My first evening in the tavern went by rapidly, and at midnight, when Pepe closed the tavern, Antonio and I were still there. Saying *"adiós"* to my new-found friends I returned to the hotel, and with my head spinning from the good wine of La Mancha wrote in my journal of my introduction to the tavern of Ramón de la Toñica.

# 8

# Village Gypsies

Though the reader may view this chapter as a digression from my experiences with Antonio the bootblack and other friends in the city, I was also meeting Gypsies who do not suffer from the racial prejudice in Guadix. Among these other Gypsies were those who lived in the villages of Benalúa and Fonelas.

I first learned that they were regarded differently from the urban Gypsies when village shopkeepers said, "Our Gypsies are not like the lazy ones of Guadix. They work the way we do. Some own land. Others work in the sugar refinery."

What I heard surprised me. Gypsies have rarely been land owners and factory workers.

The village Gypsies, in turn, said, "We live and work like Castilians." And yet, they remained Gypsies—they had not intermarried. While living among and like Castilians, they had managed to fulfill the goal Juan de Dios Ramirez in *Nosotros los Gitanos* had set forth: to benefit from Spanish society and yet to hold on to their identity.

I have divided the material in this chapter into three sub-headings: (a) an evening with the Benalúa horse traders; (b) a religious service in the same village; (c) and experiences with the bronze Gypsies of Fonelas.

**CALO IN THE BAR EL MIOCID**

In Benalúa it was the horse traders who interested me the most. One night I went into the smoke-filled bar el Miocid to look for the

77

ones the local mailman had introduced me to. The Miocid, one of several bars in the village, had a cordial owner, and the horse traders had chosen it as their gathering place. They sold and bought animals on the dirt area out front, and continued their negotiations in the bar. Later, they would gather there in the evening to drink and play cards or dominoes. They knew nothing about the meaning of Miocid, the name of the epic poem which describes the adventures of the Cid, Spain's national hero, so they gave it their own name, "*raura*," derived from "*herradura*" (horseshoe).

I joined Luis de los Caballos (Luis of the horses) at one of the tables. Slim and roguish-looking with a scraggly mustache, he had just drunk from a *porrón* (pitcher) of wine without touching the spout to his lips and passed it to Torcuato, a Gypsy in his twenties, whose red mustache was set off by a soiled, round black hat. It was then the turn of Mauro, an appealing older Gypsy with a deep, brown skin. When he shoved it in front of me, I said, "*No abello éxito tapiyando mol de este coró*," (I don't have any luck drinking from this pitcher,) using several Caló words including *coró* for pitcher.

Luis laughed. "Patience."

Drinking this way is common in Andalusia and sanitary, once mastered. Frequently, it is the only way to drink water in public places such as automobile service stations where cups are not provided. This pitcher was of glass with a handle and a long, slender nozzle. The trick was to hold it at the proper height so that on tilting, the stream

*Antonio the mailman, with the Miocid bar in the background, introduced the author to the Gypsies of Benalúa, the largest concentration of Gypsies in the region.*

from the nozzle entered the mouth. Up to now, my efforts had not been successful. I had spilled wine on my forehead, on my neck and on my shirt, and when a little wine did reach my mouth I choked on it.

We began to use Caló. Soon the other clients gathered around our table. Among them was Faustino, the knife-sharpener, who had made his living as a mule shearer at the time when there were more mules to be sheared. I was soon responding to questions from others, who were curious about this *payo* who knew Caló. The ones who could not get close called over words in Caló for me to give the meaning in Spanish.

It was all done in a friendly manner. With the directness of the Andalusian a hand would be placed on my shoulder to attract my attention, a sibilant "p-s-s-t" would sound in my ears, and a voice would enquire,

"*Qué quiere decir chaboró?*" (What does *chaboró* mean?)

"Boy," I would reply.

"*Pañí?*"

"Agua."

And so they continued with *balichón* (pork), *mol* (wine), *tatón* (bread), *chuquel* (dog), *pureta* (old woman), *jamar* (to eat), and *bal* (hair).

To questions on the meaning of such basic words, Luis and Mauro would shake their heads and say, "He knows that," implying that the others should not trouble me with trivia.

To myself I thought, "This is like taking an oral examination in Caló. But instead of being interrogated by university professors, the questions are coming from illiterate Gypsies." I was sweating from the pressure of responding with the correct Spanish word, the heavy cigarette smoke, and my consumption of wine. My situation was like an experience described by Alexandros Paspates, who collected the Romany spoken in the Ottoman Empire in his *Etudes sur Les Tching-hianes* (1870):

> I often found myself in the midst of the tents alone among a horde of Gypsies, who would press around me, hurling words at me from every side, each correcting the other...

The questions continued as the smoke thickened, and as the pitcher was passed around.

My drinking technique was improving, and I was no longer spilling wine on my shirt. Luis and Mauro encouraged me by clasping my hands whenever I correctly gave the Spanish meaning to lesser known words such as *brijindar* (to rain) and *chinclí* (key), and to terms used in animal-trading: *choró* (mule), *jel* and *jarañó* for burro. Despite the commotion around me, I took time to jot down unfamiliar words, some of which took months to unravel. (From throughout the region, and elsewhere in Spain, I eventually acquired about two hundred and seventy, down appreciably from the four thousand Borrow estimated to exist in the 1830s.)

When Mauro pronounced a word for my benefit, he moved his face to within a few inches of mine, until our noses almost touched. Although foreign to my nature, I learned to accept the invasion of my personal space, especially on meeting strange Gypsies. Getting close made establishing rapport easier. I used the technique to get acquainted with Gypsies at Madrid's *rastro*, the sprawling flea market visited by thousands of Madrileños every Sunday. I had noticed a well-dressed antique dealer of about fifty, who appeared to be a Gypsy, sitting on a stool on the sidewalk with his old coins and guns spread out on the street in front of him. I leaned over his goods, and with my face close to his, I asked in Caló, *"Tusa calé?"* (Are you a Gypsy?)

"Sí," he replied.

And then, pointing to the staff he was holding, which he used to point to his merchandise, I asked, "What do you call that in Caló?" Before he had time to reply, I said, *"Es un ran."*

His eyes opened in amazement that I knew the word, and a big smile appeared on his face. He called to two Gypsies in their upper teens, as well-dressed as he, introducing them as his nephews, and telling them that I knew Caló.

"We know little of it," they said.

"It is so," said the uncle. "And it is a shame. Among the Gypsies of Madrid and of the cities to the north there is little left of the language."

Mauro got up from the table several times, saying, *"Nahelo muclar."* (I'm going to urinate.) On one of his absences I walked toward the bar to refill the pitcher. A dark-faced Gypsy, who had been standing near us, said, "You know more Caló than I." The owner's daughter, a pretty girl in her teens, came to serve me, and I ordered a half liter of wine, topped with beer.

Luis could easily have been one of the picaroons described in the Golden Age of Spanish literature (1550-1680). I could visualize him as the Gypsy in Cervantes' *The Dogs' Colloquy* who twice sells a bobtailed burro to the same buyer, first with an artificial tail attached, and, later after stealing the burro, reselling it without its false tail. He would have carried this off, not so much for the profit, as for the pleasure he would receive in retelling the story.

I am sure that any crimes he may have committed were petty ones, but he could not resist determining if I had any money to part with. Early in our relationship he made his move, a half-hearted effort to interest me in a flamenco show to be held, if I would finance it, in the back room of the Miocid. I showed no interest, and he never approached the subject of money again.

He had the spontaneity of the Gypsies as I found when driving through the pottery-selling village of Purullena, astride the highway to Granada. I saw him walking along the side of the road with several other Gypsies, and called out, "A-a-y-y Luis!" He came running over with a big smile, shouting in Caló, as though he had not seen me for several years, "*Quiribó! Quiribó!*" (Friend! Friend!) He and his friends invited me for a drink in a nearby bar where I shared in Luis' delight — almost child-like to an Anglo-Saxon — made up of smiles, loud greetings and miscellaneous phrases in Caló and Spanish. "*Tapiyamos y jamamos tapas de balichón y bobís.*" (Let's drink and eat *tapas* of meat and lima beans.)

Mauro had a different personality. He reminded me of sturdy Carlos the smith, though not physically, because he was short whereas Carlos was tall and broad-shouldered. But they each had a quiet reserve and depth of character that their fellow villagers, Gypsy and non-Gypsy, respected. One evening Mauro asked, "Are there Gypsies in your country?"

"Yes, many, but they keep to themselves."

He shook his head in disapproval. "Not us. We live close to the Castilians. My wife and children are friendly with our *payo* neighbors. *Somos todos Benaluenses.*" (We are all residents of Benalúa.)

One spring evening at dusk when I was standing on the platform of the railroad station talking to Manolo, the station master, a small bronze figure sitting on the back of a plodding burro, both tired from working in the fields all day, came toward us. As the figure drew nearer and crossed the railroad tracks, I saw that it was Mauro, with his hoe resting on the back of the burro. "Mauro!" I shouted as did the station master. Mauro returned our greetings, continued along the dirt road leading into the village and to his cave dug into a red conical tower of earth, where his wife fattened a partridge in a cage for eating, and where she wove baskets as the Gypsies of my mother's girlhood had in Massachusetts. I wondered, with the increasing numbers of

*Mauro, who has a large vocabulary in Caló, is returning from a day of work in the Benalúa countryside. He is not as grim as he appears to be. A kind person, he is liked by all the residents of Benalúa.*

tractors and automobiles, how much longer Mauro and the other Benalúa villagers would be riding into the countryside on the backs of mules and burros. In another decade, would these animals be a rarity?

A few months later, on a Saturday morning toward the end of August, I was on my way to the *feria de ganado* (the livestock fair) in Guadix. The city was crowded, and a small boy cooking *churros*, the deep-fried dough the Guadijeños loved, was working at top speed to keep up with the demand. Along the sidewalk, which ran past the shady park, vendors were selling candy, toys and books. Perhaps Luis had returned from France where several weeks ago he had gone with his wife and ten children to harvest vegetables. I soon spotted him heading toward the market and called out to him, *"Quinamos algunos jeles de los jambusnes!"* (Let's steal some burros from the non-Gypsies!)

He replied, *"Juna! Juna! Qué viene los jundunares!"* (Look out! The police are coming!)

As we headed for the Café Bar Guadix, across from the market, the favorite drinking place of the horse traders, I looked closely at their bouncing walk, feet turned outward and legs elevated in each stride. I fell into step with them, and imitated their rangy strides. We were soon enveloped by the throng of shoppers and vendors with their cries of "Barato! Barato!" The voice of a vendor who sold a cone similar to an ice cream cone, but without ice cream, carried above the others. "M-a-r-t-i-n-o-s! M-a-r-t-i-n-o-s!" In the crowded bar, we had a glass of wine with *tapas* of tiny fish and potato salad.

We then walked to the dry bed of the river Guadix where the animal fair was held. It was a modest event compared with the famous ones of Seville and Jerez de la Frontera, but it intrigued me. There were about one hundred animals—thirty horses, the rest burros and mules. Had I been an artist, I would have spent the entire day sketching the scene before me. One white burro had a red and blue saddle blanket. Another was wearing a face harness of delicately designed leather with red blinders. A mare walked casually among the buyers and sellers followed by a bounding colt. A Castilian horse trader from Alcudia rode up in a cloud of dust kicked up by his four trotting horses. Some animals nibbled at the few pieces of greenery that had survived the hot, dry, summer, while others munched on feed thrown to them by their owners.

*This old Gypsy is one of the few to ride to the Saturday market in Guadix in a burro-drawn cart.*

Onlookers surrounded a spirited brown and white pony with a hand-tooled harness, which had just whirled up pulling a two-wheeled pony cart. Motorcycles zoomed along the gravel river bed, as hard-packed as a race track. Gypsies and non-Gypsies discussed the merits of the animals while they watched horses being put through their paces. Burros and donkeys brayed, and horses neighed. The *gitanas*—there were no Castilian women there—stood apart from the men, holding their babies on their hips. The Gypsy men assumed the set poses of subjects in the early days of photography. One of them, standing erect with an arm folded over his chest and his staff in the crook of his arm, reminded me of photographs of American Civil War generals.

Luis walked up to a heavy-set Gypsy in his late fifties who was wearing a broad-brimmed brown hat, a vest under a wrinkled coat and a staff with a long cord attached to it, introducing him as his brother, "Lata."

"I have sixteen children," Lata told me. "These are my *chaborós*," he said pointing to several nearby children. One was a bright-eyed, impish-looking boy of twelve in a red, turtle-neck sweater. Another was a boy of thirteen whose eyes stared out at me through long hair falling over his forehead.

"Put on your show!" said Lata.

The twelve-year old mounted a horse, and holding the reins in his left hand, leaned forward tapping the horse on the knee with a staff until the horse knelt. He then had him lie down. The older boy had his horse lie on its side while he sat on its flanks. Another boy had his horse nudge him with his head from behind, and then pick up a stick from the ground in its mouth.

Applauding the boys for their performance, I said, *"adíos,"* telling Luis I hoped to see him soon in the Miocid.

## RELIGIOUS SERVICE IN A GYPSY CAVE

I frequently went with the Benalúa mailman, one of the many Antonios I knew, on his daily rounds of the caves. The mail delivered, we would stop in a bar where the owner served *tapas* of hot crabs.

One day he told me that a Gypsy Protestant minister had recently arrived in the village and was holding nightly services. Since I knew that Gypsies have had little interest in formal religion, I wanted to find out what success the pastor was having. I arranged with Antonio for us to attend a service.

On the way to the pastor's cave, which served as the church, Antonio motioned toward another cave that we were approaching. "This is where Dulce lives," he said. "She is the Gypsy whose brother was killed by her ex-husband in the fight in Guadix." Antonio led me into the cave yard where eight or nine Gypsies were gathered. Dulce, a pretty girl of nineteen with a baby in her arms was among them, along with her mother and father, and neighbors. Although dressed in shabby clothing, they were a striking group, their dark eyes sparkling with life.

To Dulce I said, motioning to her baby, *"Dia! Qué jucalía!"* (How pretty!)

And then, since Gypsy custom frowned on a stranger's talking to a *gitana*, I talked with her father, courteous and dignified, who was taking calmly the loss of the son who had died for the honor of his sister. He recognized the misfortune as part of Gypsy life.

I wondered whose fault it was. The husband's? Had he tarnished her honor, thereby sullying the reputation of the family? Was this what led to her brother's death after he and his Benalúa relatives had battled with the husband's family from Alcudia? Or could it be possible that Dulce was to blame? Her name, which in English meant "soft" and "sweet," seemed to describe her perfectly. But yet...since the separation from her first husband she had not only remarried, but had again been separated. Two marriages and two separations. Was she really the sweet woman she appeared to be?

At the pastor's cave, his wife, a full-bodied *romí*, motioned to us to enter a room illuminated by a lone light bulb hanging from the ceiling. It had a dirt floor and yellow walls on which large red dots had been superimposed. It had been the living room of the previous occupants, a non-Gypsy family. Twenty-five old chairs were awaiting the congregation.

Isidoro, a tall slender Gypsy of about forty with a mustache and long sideburns, was standing beneath a wooden cross attached to the wall. He was reading the Bible. In a niche below the cross were three pamphlets, translations into Spanish of sermons by the evangelist Billy Graham. He handed us a Bible. "The reading," he said, "will be from St. Luke."

When the congregation arrived, I saw that it was mostly families of horse traders. The men walked with easy dignity to the back of the room. Luis and Mauro were not among them, but Lata, Luis' brother was. On entering the room they removed their sweat-stained hats. The wives, who sat in front with a few teenage girls and smaller children, were wearing their usual bright colors—one with a yellow sweater; another with an orange skirt. To my surprise, the teenage daughter of the pastor and two other teenagers had let their long hair fall freely to their shoulders rather than having it pulled tightly back. Perhaps it was related to their new-found faith.

Shortly after nine, everyone was seated, and with the ever-present flies of Andalusia buzzing around us, Isidoro opened the service with a brief prayer. The congregation then burst into joyous singing and shouts of "Hallelujah! Hallelujah!" There were no hymn books; the songs were memorized. The service continued with more prayers, Bible reading, singing and clapping of hands and Isidoro's sermon, which was on what makes a good heart.

Twice everyone held the hand of his neighbor, but this was too embarrassing for the thirteen-year old *chaborí* in front of me, so a middle-aged woman extended her hand. Small children wandered in and out, and one mother nursed a baby at her breast. By the end of the service—it lasted an hour—one of the men was in tears, and the pastor was sweating from his efforts. The men put on their hats and lit up cigarettes. I shook hands with Isidoro, and pressed some pesetas on him, because no offering had been taken.

A few days later, I visited him and sat with the family while they finished a meal of sausage, rice, bread and wine. He spoke freely of his religious calling, and convinced me that he was sincere. He supported his family by working as an agricultural day laborer.

"Where are you from?" I asked.

"Málaga."

"And how did you become a Protestant?"

"In Granada, I heard a French Gypsy preaching, and liked what I heard. No church sent me here. I came on my own."

I believed him. He was living like the poorest Gypsy, and his religious supplies were meager, just the few Bibles and pamphlets I had seen.

"What is your denomination?"

"*Evangelical Pentecostal*," he replied, adding that its headquarters were in Philadelphia. He could not, however, give me an address nor did he have any material from Philadelphia.

Later, I learned that many Gypsies in Spain had become evangelical Protestants. The money-changers of Badajoz told me about their newly acquired faith, and at the invitation of the *marchantes* of Avila, who sell their horses outside the walls of Saint Teresa's city, I attended their nightly service.

Isidoro and these other modern-day Protestants are having more success than George Borrow did in the 1830s when he represented the Bible Society of England. Borrow, who said that one of his goals was to enlighten the "thievish half-wild people," the Gypsies, was skeptical about the results. The *gitanas*, he wrote, valued his translation of Saint Luke into Caló, not because of its doctrine, but because of its usefulness as a charm.

Isidoro's stay, however, in Guadix was brief. A complaint was lodged against him in the court in Guadix. The substance—given to me by a friend in the court—was that he was attacking the Catholic Church. Whatever the niceties of the law concerning freedom of religious expression may have been, Isidoro, pressured by the authorities, left Benalúa and his congregation within six months after his arrival.

## THE BRONZE GYPSIES OF FONELAS

The Gypsies I admired most in the region were the bronze Gypsies of Fonelas. They are the most Gypsy-looking in the region—and perhaps in all of Spain. They have deep, bronze complexions and strong physiques. On excellent terms with the other villagers, they drink and work with them as friends and equals. The young men wear thick mustaches which make them look fierce. The women are equally striking with delicate features, soft voices, and graceful carriage. Antonio in Guadix with his olive skin and slight physique would have been out of place among the Fonelas Gypsies, none of whom he knew anyway, for there were few ties between city and village Gypsies.

The first Gypsy I met in Fonelas was in the Bar los Carmenes where I was playing dominoes with some non-Gypsies. A ferocious looking Gypsy with black skin and black hair falling to his shoulders introduced himself, saying in English, "Good evening, sir. How are you?" I was surprised. These were the first English words I had heard in the region except from Falcó and a few from Antonio the guide. They came from a Gypsy in his mid-twenties named Rafael.

"You speak English?" I said, dropping out of the domino game where I was losing money.

"A little." And it was a little. In Spanish, he told me that as a waiter in a hotel in Mallorca for two years he had learned a few phrases of English, French and German. He could say, "Good morning,"

"Good evening," "Thank you," and a few other expressions in each language.

"Are you still a waiter there?" I asked, thinking he might be on vacation.

"No!" he replied. "I hated it. I made good money, but I felt like a slave."

His comment intrigued me. I had no doubt that he was successful financially. He must have been especially attractive to the North Europeans who would have seen their ideal Spaniard in this dark, masculine Gypsy with strong, even features and flashing, white teeth.

"I will never return to Mallorca," he added. "I prefer to live freely and to work in the open air."

"But life is not easy in the village," I said.

"Ah! You know that already. It is true. My home is here, but in one year I work only a few days at a time, not over a month or two in all. So I must take my wife and child to Murcia to harvest almonds and to Jaén to harvest olives. This is my choice."

One evening in the Bar el Triunfo Rafael gave me a lesson in hospitality. He said that I was his guest, and could not pay for any wine. About eleven o'clock I became hungry, not having had any dinner, and while Rafael, who might not eat until midnight, was talking with some other friends, I ordered and paid for a pork sandwich. When he noticed it, he asked, "Why did you pay?"

"You have to work hard for your money," I replied.

"You must understand why I work. First, it is to provide for my wife and children. After that for a few luxuries. I like to smoke, to drink a little, and I have a television. These are luxuries. Another is to buy a friend drinks and a sandwich."

His hospitality wasn't limited to the bars. He invited me to his home for dinner. When I arrived at his cave, high in the Barranco Rosario, which he bought in 1979 for eight hundred dollars, the table was already set with a new table cloth and cloth napkins. His wife served a paella of rice, rabbit, peas and other vegetables. For dessert she served us oranges and bananas, and then like Isabel in Guadix, waited until we had finished before serving her child and herself.

Rafael, the thinker, fascinated me. Once, he said, "You know, when I was only fifteen I had decided for myself about Franco." Another time he said, "I am an atheist." And he named several of the people I knew in the village who were also unbelievers.

*Two of the bronze Gypsies of Fonelas, Rafael and his wife, in front of their cave. Rafael is in demand as a waiter in the tourist hotels in Mallorca, but prefers the simple life of Fonelas.*

Rafael introduced me to Manuel, a slender, wiry Gypsy in his forties, who always wore a felt hat. When I met him, he had just grasped a Castilian around the neck, and was playfully wrestling with him. He let go of his friend and walked toward me with the cat-like step of a bull fighter. He had the bronze coloration of the Fonelas Gypsies and a narrow, pointed face featuring a prominent nose. With his dark face, fine features and darting black eyes, he was a quintessential Gypsy. He realized this, and was proud of it, but his friends were more apt to be Castilian than Gypsy.

He was poor and lived in an ordinary cave with his wife and eight children, but like his fellow villagers, he had a natural dignity which lifted him above his poverty. When he emerged from his hill-side cave with his old jacket draped gracefully over his shoulders like a cloak, and began his descent along the trash-littered path to the ravine below, I was reminded that Washington Irving noted in *Tales of the Alhambra* that poverty to the Spaniard was not a disgrace. Manuel looked like an hidalgo.

Another Gypsy friend was Camilo, a big man, who like Manuel, knew Caló and had a large family. When he learned of my interest in Caló he invited me to his house, which he had built in 1970 on the site of a cave, to add to my vocabulary. One of the two Gypsy-owned houses in the village, it had a tin roof and walls of cinder block and brick, painted white. When I arrived the family was sitting in the front yard weaving chair seats from esparto grass while listening to flamenco on the Granada radio.

*This is where the highly-regarded Fonelas Gypsy Camilo prefers to be, alongside his wife in the heart of the family. Here the family is weaving chair seats of esparto grass.*

The two oldest sons, both in their upper teens, were striking-looking youths, powerfully built like their father, and wearing long sideburns and mustaches. One of them was leaving in a few days with his wife to spend four months in Murcia picking tomatoes. They observed me as I did them. Several years later one of them said to me, "I see that you are wearing the same trousers." Antonia, a slender sixteen year old with delicate features and chocolate skin, was Indian-looking like her mother Luisa, a plump *gitana* wearing dangling earrings whose black hair was drawn tightly back and braided in a pony tail.

Camilo loved Fonelas and its countryside where he worked as a day laborer and sometimes raised his own crops on rented land. He supplemented his income by gathering wild products such as esparto grass and caper berries. He once showed me an edible thistle, and cut me a piece to try. It had a clean, dry taste. Then, pointing to a grove of alamo trees along the river, he said, "I don't see how anyone could not like this." I nodded in approval, although this semi-arid country with its brown, treeless ridges would not appeal to everyone.

Because they loved the land, I could not picture Camilo and the other Gypsies of Fonelas living in the city and shining shoes or selling lottery tickets. Like the Gypsies of Benalúa, they had gone beyond just working on the land. Hungering to possess it as much as their non-Gypsy villagers, twelve of them, with money saved from working outside the region, had bought land to cultivate.

Pepe del Bigote, so called because of a thick, black mustache, who was half-Gypsy and half-Castilian, invited me to explore some caves with him and Camilo. He called them "Moorish caves" as did the other villagers, but bronze-age man had built them.

We drove a few miles south of Fonelas on a dirt road past fields of sugar beets, corn, wheat, tobacco, and tomatoes and orchards of apple, peach, cherry and plum trees. At an abandoned farm, Pepe started rapidly up toward the base of a high cliff where the caves were located. Leaving the grass and scree, he climbed along a narrow ledge, which led to a cave room. He then entered a tunnel. I followed. Strugling on my hands and knees in a hole in the ground had never appealed to me. Camilo felt the same way, and he called out, *"Pepe, dónde va?"*

Pepe replied, "Up."

But how could he go up, I wondered, while still in the tunnel? After I crawled a few more feet, feeling in front of me to avoid striking my head, I heard a scraping sound above, and felt particles of dirt falling down. Pepe had found an exit from the tunnel.

"It's a stairway," he shouted. "Come on up!"

Groping with my hands, I felt a series of steps which had been cut into the earth. I called to Camilo, "Come slowly!"

Putting his hands on the steps to show their location, I then climbed upwards, still in darkness. The steps—fifteen in all—did not go straight up, but wound around, forming a circular staircase in the heart of the earth. They led to a room with the front wall open where Pepe was smoking a cigarette, and rearranging the black mustache which gave him the look of a robber chief. When Camilo joined us, we sat for a few minutes looking out over the wide valley of the Fardes, enjoying the view as bronze-age man had done four thousand years ago.

On returning to the village, we passed an irrigation channel in which village women, Gypsies and non-Gypsies, were washing clothes while chatting merrily together. To quench our thirst we stopped at the Bar Nuevo for a glass of wine. Manolo the owner served us cod fish cooked in tomato sauce.

The residents of Fonelas are aware that Gypsies in Guadix and elsewhere in Spain usually have different work and social habits from the ones in Fonelas, and that they do not have the relationship with Castilians that exists in Fonelas. When I spoke about my country to a group of students, ten and eleven years old—no Gypsies were present, because they drop out after the second grade—one student asked, "Are the Gypsies like the negroes in America?"

One of my friends was Gilberto, a Castilian day laborer, who lived with his plump wife and three children in a cave next to a Gypsy family. He had a round, red face set off by prominent ears. With his short height and broad shoulders, he looked like his Celto-Iberian ancestors as did Pepe el Pando. He could not read or write, but he had a good mind and could express himself well. In the Bar Nuevo he had said to me in front of Camilo and Manuel, "Fonelas is not pretty. It has no luxuries, but it is a good pueblo—and all of us are friends." The others nodded in agreement.

He took me to visit dolmens above the village where bronze-age man had buried his dead. One day I went with him to a later-day burial ground, the village cemetery, where he had dug the grave for a neighbor who had just died.

Not wishing to be present during the grave-side ceremony, I started down the trail. As the mourners drew closer, I noticed that they were not wearing long faces, but joyful expressions as though attending a fiesta. Among them were two or three Gypsy families. One of the Gypsy men, whom I knew only casually, saw me as an old friend under the glow of his alcoholic consumption. Hurling himself at me, he grasped my hand, thrust his face into mine, shouting, "*Ola amigo! Qué tal?*"

Returning his handshake, I replied with a loud, "*Qué hay! Qué pasa?*" I looked into his eyes which were so close that I could hardly focus on them. He then withdrew a step or two, and still holding my hand, looked around at the other Gypsies who were smiling and giving me their greetings. He reached down and picked up a lovely, chocolate-faced girl of about two, dressed in a short smock with a bare bottom. Proudly holding her in his arms, he said, "*Es mi chaborí.*"

"How pretty!" I said.

"I made her with my *cal*," he said, using the Caló word for male genitals.

It was now my turn to reply. The Gypsies, *rom* and *romí*, gathered around me, awaiting my response. If I indicated that I didn't know what *cal* meant the others would be amused, not to poke fun at me but just because it was a humorous situation. So without hesitating I said, *"Yo sé. Con tu cal en el jojoi de tu romí."* (I know. With your *cal* in your wife.)

Everyone laughed as they continued up the trail, *gitanas* as well as *gitanos*. They were surprised, but pleased that I had understood.

I liked walking along the edge of the mesa above the cave-lined ravines where a cool breeze blows and the summer heat is left below. The Arab peak, Cerro Mencal, is close at hand, and the distant Sierra Nevada comes into view.

On one of my strolls, to get a better view of the caves below, I walked out onto a narrow butte. Two boys, one about seven wearing a cowboy hat, popped up from a cave below, shouting, *"Hola! Hola!"*

"Where is your cave?" I asked.

"Right there," they replied, pointing toward the rim. Looking down, I saw the entrance to a cave opening onto a narrow ledge. The childrens' mother, was hanging clothes on a line to dry. On seeing me, she scrambled up to where we were standing. She was an attractive

*A Gypsy family on the ridge above their cave.*

woman with a chocolate skin, but was badly crippled in one leg. She shared the cave with her mother while her husband was away in Almería working on construction.

"I like the view from here," I said.

"Not I," she replied. "It is very ugly. No trees. No grass. Just dirt. And caves, caves, caves!"

While we were talking, an old Castilian with a bad eye and a stubble of beard on his face walked slowly toward us from another cave. He was using a cane for support and wearing a vest even in the hot sun. "*Hola Juanita*," he said.

Without acknowledging his greeting Juanita immediately began to tease him. "You are a *payo*," she said in a stern voice.

The old man, leaning on his cane, chuckled and nodded his head.

"And you are *malo* (bad)," she continued.

The old man chuckled some more.

"And you, too, she said, looking at me. "You are a *payo*, but I'm a Gypsy, better than you two."

I came to two black-haired *chaborós* about thirteen years old kicking a ball. When they learned I was an American, they asked to see my money. Was it just an innocent request? Or did they plan to beg from me? If so, I would be disappointed, because Fonelas was the only village where Gypsies had not asked for money. I took out my billfold—I had no loose change—pulled out a dollar bill, and put it in their hands. They excitedly admired it, turned it over, and then politely returned the bill to me. My faith in the Gypsies of Fonelas remained intact.

# 9

# Fishing for Birds

On a cool fall afternoon, I went along with Antonio, Joselito and the son of Black Beret to climb the Gypsy peak, Cerro de la Bala. We walked up the trail beyond Antonio's cave, and cut up sharply to the left to the base of one of the steep ridges leading to the summit. Climbing directly up the ridge, using our hands on the soft rock to maintain our balance, we passed several abandoned caves nestled on barely accessible man-made terraces, and shortly above them arrived on the small summit plateau. Although it had taken only ten minutes or so from Antonio's cave to get there, the view of the Sierra Nevada and the sheer drop-offs on the edge of the plateau gave me the feeling of having scaled a major peak.

I had been on Cerro de la Bala before and watched teen-aged boys flying kites and small children playing tag, unconcerned over the eroding edges of the plateau where a false step would have led to a bad fall. But this time, there was something different taking place. A middle-aged man was standing alone at one end of the plateau, waving a twenty-foot long bamboo pole in the air with outstretched arms.

"What is he doing?" I asked Antonio.

"*Es un pescador de avión*," (He is a fisher of airplanes,) he replied.

This made no sense to me. So I asked Antonio what he meant. But even as I asked the question, I began to understand. Large, dark-colored birds—at first I thought they were hawks—were flying over the plateau, sometimes swooping down to fifteen or twenty feet above our heads to catch flies. These were the *"aviones,"* apparently the local name for the bird. And the man had attached to the end of his pole an open noose tied in a slip knot. He tried to hold the pole so that a bird would fly into the noose and be caught when the knot tightened. So the man was indeed a "fisher of birds."

His equipment and motions were similar to the fisherman who fishes in streams and lakes. My guess is that this has been a well-established sport among the cave dwellers for hundreds of years, and was perhaps known to the Celto-Iberians who lived amongst these hills long before the arrival of the Romans and the Moors.

Washington Irving in *Tales of the Alhambra* tells how he, too, was puzzled at first on observing "aerial fishermen," as he called them, waving their long poles at birds. The fishing grounds, though, of Irving's fishermen were not the hills above Guadix, but the towers and battlements of the Alhambra.

It was a trying sport, because the long pole was awkward to handle and the sportsman became tired from holding his arms fully extended while supporting the weight of the pole. There was also an element of danger. I noticed that the *pescador* was standing at the very edge of the plateau, which dropped off at that point about seventy-five feet straight down before leveling off at a shelf. A slight miscalculation while maneuvering the pole could lead to a fall.

Later, when I saw other *pescadores* in action, I noted that they, too, were always near the edge of the plateau rather than safely located in the middle. The explanation, I thought, must have something to do with the drafts that shot up the sides of these peaks, with flies being lifted along with the air flows. Since the birds were after the flies, they would be darting over the updrafts.

After we had been there for about thirty minutes, the *pescador's* noose tightened around a bird, a fly catcher of some kind, bluish black and about six inches long. I later identified it with the aid of a school teacher in Guadix who gave me its Latin name, *Delichon Urbica* or house martin, not related, as I first supposed, to the North American purple martin.

"We eat these birds, sometimes," Antonio said. "Fried, they are tough. If boiled for a long time, they make a soup that isn't bad."

"That's right," said the *pescador*. "I hope to catch one or two more to go into a soup."

As I looked closer at him, I saw that he looked familiar. It turned out he was a brother of my drinking companion Pedro el Moro in the bar of Ramón de la Toñica, and had the same dark skin as his brother and the same strongly chiseled features.

"I have been fishing most of my life," he said. "I began as a boy for the thrill of climbing Cerro de la Bala and looping an occasional bird. It is still a sport for me, but since I have a wife and children, my catch helps to feed us. Some of my friends, though, fish only for the excitement, throwing away the birds once caught."

For the benefit of bird lovers, I should point out that the *pescadores* or *cazadores* (hunters) as they are also called, catch only a few birds, so that the martin population is in no danger of becoming an endangered species — at least, not from the fishers of Guadix.

Another method of catching birds was to snare them, a practice at which Ambrosio in the bar of Ramón was highly skilled. I went along with him and several others into the countryside late one afternoon. We made camp near a flowing stream, drank wine, built a fire and cooked a rabbit. Before going to bed, Ambrosio placed a net on a wide flat stone in a shallow part of the stream favored by birds for drinking. Attaching a line to the net, he extended it to a clump of bushes that offered him a good view of the snare and concealment from the birds. Early the next morning, he manned the line, and jerked it tight when it was full of birds, snaring several goldfinch, sparrows and bullfinch. We plucked and broiled them for breakfast.

"When I snare more," Ambrosio said, "I sell them to owners of bars in the city. They fry them in olive oil and serve them hot to clients for a few pesetas each. Sometimes I give the goldfinches to friends, because they are good singers."

Other game in the region included rabbits, partridge and foxes. Gypsies like to hunt, but are seldom granted permission by the Guardia Civil to carry firearms, because of the belief that Gypsies are irresponsible. There are ways, though, of catching rabbits without rifles. A dark-skinned cousin of Antonio told me about a technique he used. "I keep a live ferret in a cage in my cave. When I go hunting, I take the ferret along and on finding a promising looking hole, drop the ferret in. I then place a large net over the hole. When the rabbit tries to escape the ferret and leaves his home, he gets entangled in the net, and I have rabbit for dinner."

Camilo, my Gypsy friend in Fonelas, told me about two other methods of catching rabbits. "You see this," he said, taking down a steel trap from the wall of his cave. "I set it without bait along rabbit runways, and cover it with loose soil, leaves and brush so that the rabbit doesn't know it is there."

Despite their being much sought after, rabbits are still plentiful, and in my hikes in the countryside I often saw them dashing into the shelter of bushes at my approach. Carthaginian traders, three thousand years ago, had also seen the rabbits bounding about the landscape. They were so impressed with them that they called the country Spania, the land of rabbits. They continue to be a convenient food in a region where most people cannot afford fresh meat in their daily diet. Because the terrain and climate of Guadix are ideal for them, it is possible that without the continued hunting of the rabbits, they would become the pests that they are in Australia.

A favorite activity of cave children was catching scorpions which thrive in the summer months of dry, hot weather similar to the American Southwest. Joselito and I had a lesson in this sport from a Castilian boy of fourteen, who lived with his family in a large, comfortable cave just above the economic frontier. We had become bored with watching a Spanish camera crew shooting a film of the caves for a Madrid television station, so casting about for something more interesting to do, the boy suggested we hunt for scorpions. We all agreed that it was a good idea, Joselito jumping up and down to show his enthusiasm.

"The first thing to do," the boy said, "is to find a scorpion hole."

This wasn't too difficult, because scorpions were plentiful anywhere off the beaten path. The holes are about the diameter of a pencil and the dirt is smooth on the edges where the scorpion comes and goes.

"Now," he continued, "we pour water into the hole until the scorpion comes out."

Finding a likely looking hole, though, was not enough. The scorpion must be at home and not out for a stroll. We spent about an hour filling holes with water without success. This meant much running back and forth to fetch water from the nearest spigot, about fifty yards away. I was beginning to be impatient, but Joselito and the Castilian boy kept their enthusiasm. Their patience was finally rewarded when they found two scorpions at home. The first was caught in a can for later displaying to friends; the second was dispatched with stones. We had to be careful for though the sting from their tails isn't fatal, it is painful.

Antonio had told me that a person who has *gracia* can pick up a scorpion with umpunity. If stung he will feel no pain. The actions of the Castilian boy, however, indicated that he did not have *gracia*; he treated scorpions with respect.

Young cave dwellers are deprived of tree climbing, a sport adored by children who live in more temperate climates and where trees are permitted to grow. I spent many happy hours as a boy swinging in birch trees. But the cave children have another outlet. The ridges, knolls and miniature peaks that dominate the terrain are their natural playground. They scurry up and down them as relaxed as though rolling on grass-covered lawns. I have seen children of six or seven casually scrambling up crumbling walls that a skilled alpinist would hesitate to attempt without the use of a rope.

High on the crest of one of these ridges, I had an experience that would have caused shudders to run up and down the spine of an archeologist. A Castilian youth, on entering Antonio's cave one afternoon, showed us two arrow heads that he had recently discovered. He offered to take us where he had found them. So Antonio and I, with Joselito tagging along, followed him to the ridge in which his cave and several others were dug. The ridge had a sheer face about sixty feet high on the side of the caves. "We have to climb to the top of it," our guide said. "But the face is too steep." He led us along its base beyond the last cave until we could get onto the ridge. The ridge soon steepened and we had to move carefully. The crumbly earth added to the precariousness of the ascent. But while I was watching my every step, Joselito was bounding along, practically running up my back.

At the highest point of the ridge, almost directly above the Castilian's cave, and where it fell away sharply on each side, he pointed down toward his feet.

"Here! Look!"

I looked, and to my amazement, saw two human bones sticking out of the earth. Before I could say a word, Joselito had seized one, a forearm and thrown it with a shout of glee, so it went rattling down the face of the ridge. Antonio, digging with his hands, came up with another arrow head. I put my hands into the soft earth and in a few moments discovered several ceramic fragments. It came to me at once. We were standing on an ancient burial site, probably of the Bronze Age. The region abounds in the remains of ancient man.

The area had originally been a plateau or a gentle slope but with the same magnificent view of the river below and the mountains beyond that we had that day. Man of four thousand years ago had selected this site because it had appealed to his sense of beauty. Through the centuries, the plateau had eroded into separate ridges like the one we were standing on, slowly uncovering the artifacts we had found.

Our perch was so precarious that we could stay there for only a few minutes—we were using knees and hands to maintain our balance. I started to descend and the others followed. A few times, I put out a hand to guide Joselito, but he was doing well by himself and shrugged me away. We were soon down safely with the ancient remains far above us, once again in their isolation of several thousand years.

I can already hear questions about this incident. Didn't I deliver a short lecture to the group about the need to preserve archeological sites? That artifacts should not be disturbed? The answer is that I did not, because the site was such that it would soon be eroded away by winter rains and wind. Also, it seemed unlikely that anyone from the pre-history department at the University of Granada would have the time to observe and record it.

Besides scorpion hunting and climbing ridges, Gypsy children have other pursuits as they grow older. Joselito, at five, was already learning from *payo* and Gypsy playmates his age and older how to play soccer or *fútbol*, Spain's national sport. Almost any size ball was adequate to kick around on small flat pieces of ground among the caves where the boys played until, stirring up too much dust, they were chased away by neighbors. Boys also flew kites. Spotting, harassing and begging from tourists and other visitors to the cave sector was a standard pastime for both Gypsy and Castilian children, although Joselito had not yet been introduced to this sport.

The children didn't have some of the other amusements that I had expected to see them engaged in. There was no basketball, and none of the outdoor bowling games, popular in the French countryside. And I never saw children playing at bullfighting. This was because Granada province is too mountainous to raise bulls for boys to fight clandestinely at night as they do in Seville province. So none of the Gypsy bull-fighters, such as el Gallo and Joselito, considered by Hemingway to be the greatest of Spain's *toreros*, came from Guadix.

The Gypsies of Guadix, however, carried on another tradition— dancing and singing. On a Sunday afternoon of a chilly spring day, I was sitting in the courtyard of the cave of nineteen-year-old Paco, a nephew of Antonio who was there with Isabel. We were bathed in the sunlight, reflected from the whitewashed front of the cave. The gathering was a family celebration of the christening of Paco's daughter. When I arrived, Paco was dancing, holding his body straight, as a good *bailador* should, arms over his head and fingers rhythmically snapping. He had become so hot that he had removed his shirt and was naked from the waist up. Several of his male relatives provided the *jaleo*, or accompaniment, encouraging him with shouts of "Olé."

Music came from old records played on a battered phonograph. There was no guitar, for few Gypsies in Guadix could play it. Each man took a turn dancing as the spirit moved them. When Paco became tired, a husky Gypsy with long sideburns replaced him. He could sing as well as dance and would pause, throw his head back and burst into a frenzied phrase of flamenco.

A fascinating sport was exploring old caves. With the poet from Barcelona, I visited the Cave of the Monk, a two-story cave high in the bluffs on the other side of the river from Guadix. On the interior walls we saw flakes of paint, which in our imagination confirmed the tradition that a hermit monk had once lived there.

Cave exploring was dangerous, not just because of the possibility of a roof collapsing, but because it was often necessary to scramble in exposed positions to reach the entrances to the caves. I sometimes found myself half-way up a cliff face wearing only street shoes, because the expedition was a spur-of-the-moment affair, planned only a short time before in one of the bars. Fortunately, I never joined a group seeking Roman or Moorish gold supposedly hidden in the caves. On one of these expeditions, several of my friends from Fonelas had a falling out and fought among themselves with shovels.

Travellers to distant regions assume that the natives do not appreciate the natural beauties surrounding them. They base their belief on the assumption that the local people have become immune to these features because of their long exposure to them, or that their lack of esthetic training prevents their enjoying nature's gifts. There probably are such people in the world, and there may be some among the *cueveros* of Guadix, but most *Guadijeños* are aware of their natural environment with its splendid view of the Sierra Nevada. It is not unusual to see a man climb to the summit of Cerro de la Bala, or just to the crest of the knoll in which his cave is dug, to sit alone, gazing at the outlines of the distant peaks looming beyond the high mesa, lost in the tranquility of the moment.

# 10

# The Gypsy Prince

Their principal occupation is the
manufacture and sale of iron articles,
forged by themselves.

THE STATE OF THE GYPSIES IN SPAIN (1818)
*R. Bright*

I had known Carlos the smith for a year or so, and while I liked and respected him I had never thought of him as a prince, but one morning Miguel the waiter, during a conversation over breakfast, said something which caused me to see Carlos in a different light. We had been discussing the Gypsies, most of whom Miguel knew, because he had grown up in the city of caves where his playmates were Gypsies.

"The Gypsies," he said, "*no se preocupan.* (don't trouble themselves with anything.) Take Carlos, for example, whose cave is near my home. He works one day at his *fragua* (forge), then goes several days without working. He gets up in the morning when he wants to, talks all day long to members of his family, spends his evenings at the tavern of Ramón de la Toñica, and goes to bed when he feels like it. He eats only when he is hungry, and if there is nothing but bread, that is what he has—and is satisfied. If there is no wine, he drinks water—and is satisfied." (Miguel himself drank a bottle of wine with his dinner.)

Summarizing his view of Carlos, he said, *"Vive como un príncipe!"* (He lives like a prince!)

Miguel could not read, so he was unaware that he shared Lorca's view that the Gypsies were the most aristocratic element in Spain.

Miguel had taken me by surprise—comparing Carlos, a smith, with a prince. So that evening I decided to take a closer look at Carlos at the tavern of Ramón where I frequently drank with him.

En route to the tavern, I remembered that the chiefs who led the Gypsies into the Iberian peninsula passed as royalty on their arrival. Thomas, Count of Little Egypt, entered Zaragoza in 1425, and was hospitably received by Alphonse V of Aragón. A Count James visited Andújar in 1470 with his wife Countess Louise. There was even a duke or two, but they all disappeared from the printed page in a short time. I could not, then, hope to find a genuine Gypsy prince in the twentieth century, but perhaps I could better understand Miguel's remarks.

Since it was a cool, winter evening, everyone was inside when I arrived at the tavern. Walking down two steps into the main room, I greeted several clients and Pepe, the owner, who was standing behind the wooden bar, and ordered a half litre of wine. In the cave-TV room several clients were watching an American movie with dubbed in Spanish. I continued to the next room farther into the earth, where Carlos and two of my other drinking companions, Pedro el Moro and Pepe el Pando, were watching a card game. The three of them, along with myself, now made up a *tertulia*, a group of men meeting regularly to talk, often in an exclusive men's club. Our club, the tavern of Ramón, was also exclusive, for it excluded the dwellers of the city below.

Carlos and the others were engaged in some mild horseplay. Carlos was saying to Pepe, "You are a fat one." This did not upset Pepe, so Carlos said, "You are both *payos*," implying that they were inferior to him.

Neither Pedro nor Pepe objected to Carlos' calling them a *payo*. They knew that he used it as a term of affection, although they were aware that it could have an unpleasant meaning if used in earnest to disparage non-Gypsies. Pedro, though, continuing with the joking, said, "But don't call me the '*Payo de Autopsia*,'" referring to the name the Gypsies had given to the city official who cut the rope from which a *gitana* had hanged herself in her cave.

Pedro then began to tease Carlos. Pointing to the brown hat that Carlos always wore, he asked, *"Compadre,"* do you ever take that hat off?"

It was a good question. I had wondered about the hat, too. I was so accustomed to seeing Carlos with his hat on that once when he took it off to show me a new hair-cut, I felt embarrassed seing his head exposed.

Carlos replied to Pedro, "Only when I sleep with my wife."

I offered them some wine from my pitcher, but they had their own half litres and declined. Carlos was a light drinker. Sipping the la Mancha wine from his small glass as though it were a fine liqueur, his pitcher would probably last the entire evening. Pedro and Pepe drank more, but they were not heavy drinkers either.

Carlos was in his upper fifties. He had a deeply creased, honest-looking face. His most prominent features were a strong, broad nose and a reddish-brown skin, the kind associated with the American Indian. He was standing in an easy, erect position, not leaning against a wine keg as I was doing. I suppose that his carriage could be considered a princely attribute. The German art critic Meier Graefe early in this century, when visiting the Gypsies of Sacromonte in Granada, wrote that Gypsy children, even when in rags, looked like princes and princesses. Carlos' noble bearing had been noted by the city's shopkeepers. The owner of the jewelry store in front of which Carlos displayed his wares said to me, "Carlos and other Gypsies carry themselves gracefully by instinct, whereas we have to be taught it."

From a distance, Carlos always seemed to be well dressed. Closer up, though, one saw flaws. In true Gypsy style, his clothes were never pressed. Sometimes he wore a wool jacket, a kind of sports coat, with a turtle neck sweater, but tonight he was wearing a blue, pin-striped suit with a vest and, since the weather was cool, a blue flannel shirt.

"Carlos," I said. "You look like a banker."

He chuckled, pleased at my comment, but replied in his deep voice, "I don't want to be a banker."

Meanwhile, Pepe el Pando had finished making a hand-rolled cigarette — no one else I knew rolled his own — and was arranging on top of a wine cask some snacks which he had brought up from his stall in the market: cucumbers, peppers, tomatoes and bread. A man of few words, Pepe invited us to help ourselves by pointing to the food with his head and hand.

Later that evening after the card game broke up, two Gypsies in their late teens began to wrestle in fun, something that the owner did not permit. Carlos quietly told them to stop. When they didn't, he calmly picked them up, one in each arm, held them there for a second with his strong smith muscles, and then dropped them easily to the floor. He did this while maintaining his dignity, and without hurting the two young men, who smiled and walked away. Another time when I had brought up American cigarettes for friends who had helped me with Caló and several young Gypsies gathered around me asking some for themselves, Carlos said, "No more!" That ended their requests.

Carlos, like many other Gypsies, had a limited knowledge of Caló, probably not knowing more than thirty to forty words. "We just didn't use it in our family." This did not trouble him and he felt no less Gypsy because of it. One day, though, I learned a new expression from him. We had been chatting on the main street where he had his wares displayed. It was almost two o'clock, the hour when the shops closed and the store owners and customers went home for lunch. Carlos said, *"Tengo que nahelar a la cueva. Es la hora de la jalancia."* (I have to return to the cave. It is time for eating.) He had coined *jalancia* from *jalar* (to eat.)

To know Carlos better, I decided to visit him at his forge, which was located in a cave high in the city of caves just under the summit of Cerro de la Bala. There he hammered out tools and other objects for household and agricultural use as Gypsies had done ever since entering Spain. From near the tavern, I walked along a wide ravine, the walls of which were lined with two or three levels of caves. Following the ravine until coming to a flat dusty area where children kicked soccer balls, I turned sharply upward, skirting the base of a series of cliffs that shot up to the summit of Cerro de la Bala.

In one cave a young Gypsy couple was eating from a blackened cooking pot. "Would you like to eat?" the man asked. I followed proper etiquette in replying, *"Buen provecho."* (Good eating.) I continued along the trail until challenged by an old *gitana* sitting on a broken-down chair outside her cave. At that moment a fair complexioned *gitana*, breast-feeding a new baby, appeared at her side. It was Isabeth, the former maid at the hotel. Despite my criticism of her cleaning ability, I must have made a favorable impression on her, because when she whispered in the old woman's ear, her aggressive expression softened. Isabeth had convinced her that I was not a hostile intruder.

At Carlos' forge were several children from neighboring caves, fascinated with the sight of the hot coals, the smoke and the sparks leaping from the red-hot iron, just as children are everywhere. I remember how thrilled I was as a boy looking in at the village blacksmith shop on the way to school.

Carlos' wife and a small son were with him, working as a unit. Carlos dominated the scene, but the others were doing their share. His son was pumping the bellows, and his wife pounding the hot iron, blow for blow with Carlos. Her mallet was smaller than his, but she was striking as hard as he. I had never seen a woman delivering such severe strokes. It was all the more remarkable because, although she was sturdily built like most *gitanas*, she was also feminine appearing. It was hot work, physically demanding, and they were sweating.

Carlos acknowledged my arrival, but it wasn't a time for conversation. The pieces of metal were hot and ready for shaping. They had to be worked fast. They were to be pounded into trowels, shears and other tools. The cave was full of smoke (the natural draft up the chimney was not removing all of it) and the air was so foul that my eyes were soon smarting. This, combined with the bangings reverberating off the cave walls, limited my visit to only a few minutes.

I said, "*Adiós*," and hurried down the steep trail to the bar of Ramón de la Toñica where Pedro el Moro told me that in his youth there were at least twelve Gypsy smiths. "I used to visit their forges with my friends. Soon there will be none."

Pedro was right, but I have my souvenirs. Carlos made me a pair of tongs which I use for re-arranging pieces of charcoal when cooking on my hibachi at home, and a shovel for cleaning the ashes out of my fireplace.

*Carlos the prince shaking hands with the author in front of the indoor market. Near here, he sold his hand-forged articles of iron before his cataract operation.*

Carlos and two brothers, also smiths, sold their wares on the highway to Almería, each with his own position on the sidewalk to display his merchandise. By the end of the 1970s, though, there was so little demand for their product that they displayed their wares only on Saturdays. But Monday through Friday they continued to take up their customary positions as they had for many years even though they had no goods on display.

To me, this was a sad development. For the smith, like the *marchante*, had special skills that set him apart from the other Gypsies. And in the history of the Gypsies, the profession of smith is as old or older than that of *marchante*.

About eight o'clock one evening some weeks after visiting Carlos' forge, I was approaching the tavern of Ramón to have a glass of wine before dinner. I heard someone calling, *"Hola amigo! Americano!"* Turning around, I saw Rafael, a nineteen year old nephew of Carlos, standing in front of Carlos' cave, beckoning me to join him. He had a dark, round face and the Gypsy's penetrating look and quick movements. He made his living in the market area delivering heavy sacks of grain in a push cart. A blithe spirit, he was always ready to stop to chat, even when pushing a heavy load.

*"Tiene praja?"* (Any cigarettes?) he asked with a smile as I shook his hand. His request for cigarettes and his use of the Caló word for tobacco went back to an evening in the tavern before he knew me. Not realizing I understood Caló, he had said to Carlos in an aside, *"Este payo tiene praja?"* (Does this *payo* have cigarettes?)

When he hailed me, Rafael had been enjoying the outdoor fire that was a nightly affair with Carlos' family. Although no longer used for cooking, it was a tie with the family's nomadic past, and the Caló word for the fire, *yaquí*, was still part of their limited Romany vocabulary.

"Come see where we have put the photographs you took of us," said Carlos, walking to the cave.

His wife, known as la Piranza, came with us. A pleasant person with a deep brown skin like Carlos, she had a roundish face, and wore her black hair parted on the side. With her blue skirt, pink blouse, black shawl, and silver earrings she could well have been one of the wives of the various "Counts of Egypt" who entered Spain in the fifteenth century.

She had married Carlos when he was seventeen and she fifteen. They now had nine children and twenty grandchildren. There was no doubt about her love for Carlos. It was plain to see from the warm looks she gave him. And he displayed similar feelings toward her. I told them how in my country I often thought of Carlos. Their faces lit up, and Carlos said that he, too, thought about me, even when they had been on Mallorca with their grown children. They hadn't liked Mallorca. "Too many people and automobiles." So they had returned to Guadix.

Carlos' older son, el Moro, was at the campfire. With the strong physique of his father, and the same noble carriage, he was a conspicuous figure in the city of houses where he sold lottery tickets and shined shoes, announcing his services in a deep, sonorous voice. He had a dry sense of humor, and sometimes when meeting a non-Gypsy acquaintance would greet him with, *"Hola, payo!"*

The other, Juan Carlos, was a handsome youth with a bronze skin and aquiline nose. Before I knew that he was the son of Carlos, I had seen him soliciting shoe shines in city bars in an unpleasant manner. When he felt a tip was not big enough, he would say so. I even saw him begging money, telling people that he was hungry while rubbing his stomach. He shined my shoes once, but was so disagreeable that I didn't have him shine them again for a long time. Later, I realized that he was going through a period of growth and adjustment while trying to establish himself in the overcrowded shoe-shine business.

The change in our relationship came in Ramón de la Toñica's. I was talking with Carlos when Juan walked in. Carlos introduced him as "my son." Juan and I were both taken aback, Juan because he hadn't realized that I was a friend of his father, and I because I hadn't known that Carlos was his father. From that moment on, Juan became a well-behaved teen-ager toward me. When we met a week or so later near the Plaza de Abastos in the Bar el Canario, he proudly offered to buy me a drink. I accepted, enjoying the look of pleasure that came over his face.

During the next few years, Juan outgrew his surliness to become a pleasant young man. One day in the summer of 1977, while shining my shoes, he told me that he was preparing to give up his efforts to make a living in Guadix and go to Mallorca where his sister had found him a job in a hotel.

I invited him and a Gypsy named Luis to have coffee with me in a new bar that had opened that spring, El Gallo Rojo. It was bright and spacious with lots of shining metal, and large plate-glass windows. The owner, who had worked twelve years in Germany accumulating the necessary capital for the investment, was sympathetic toward Gypsies and knew the German word, *Zigeuner*, for them. We ordered *café con leche* from one of the two Castilian boys wearing clean white jackets and black ties. If we had ordered wine we would have received free *tapas*, prepared by the owner's wife who prided herself on her *tapas*, even procuring such specialities as quail for which they made a modest charge.

"Juan," I said, "Why don't you sing flamenco in Palma de Mallorca? You're a model Gypsy. You could earn a lot of *jailleres*."

He slid off the bar stool, pulled a comb from his pocket, stood in front of a long mirror on a column near the bar, combed his coal-black hair which fell to his collar, and then assumed the classical pose of the flamenco dancer, one arm bent over his head, one hand on his hip.

"*Ole! Olé!*" I shouted, and Luis, who had an unexpectedly fine voice, sang a Gypsy song.

I had second thoughts about my suggestion. During the years of the Franco regime spontaneous dancing and singing in bars was prohibited. The owner of this bar, though, showed no concern, so I said nothing to inhibit Juan, who dashed to the juke box to select a number reasonably close to flamenco. When the music came on, he began to dance and Luis continued to sing. I kept up my "*oles*," and danced a few steps, joined by the bar owner. Clients nodded their heads in approval. The owner's wife from the back room watched the performance with a smile. Juan had chosen a sad number called "*Qué pasa con los gitanos?*" (What's with the Gypsies?) It was popular in the region that summer among both Castilians and Gypsies. We all sang along with the recorded voice:

> Gypsies are uglier
> But they eat noodles gracefully.
> Before, they cooked with wood
> Now they cook with butane.
> What is it with the Gypsies
> That once we understand ourselves
> We get along with them like brothers?

As I had observed Carlos and the other smiths and their children more closely, I began to understand Miguel's viewpoint on their living like princes. To Miguel, who worked seven days a week to provide for his wife and children, it was frustrating to have a neighbor who was unconcerned about following a fixed work schedule, and who was satisfied with a meal of only bread and water. Who but an impoverished hidalgo, or perhaps a prince in exile would have this attitude? Miguel, despite his envy of Carlos' way of living, liked him. He would have agreed that, although Carlos had neither gold nor silver, he had a rich principality in his family.

[In the winter of 1977, Carlos had cataract operations on both eyes in a hospital in Granada. He lost the sight of one eye and had to wear a thick lens on the other. He still had the strength to swing a mallet, but because of this poor eyesight could not longer work at the *fragua*. Soon his brothers could no longer work. An era, which had begun in 1489 when Ferdinand and Isabella drove the Moors from the city and the Gypsies arrived, had ended. No Lorca would again visualize the smiths as lighting the evening darkness by striking out arrows and suns on their forges.]

# 11

# The Evil Eye Death

Antonio had fallen from his bicycle when peddling from his cave down the trail, slippery from a late winter rain. He had injured a shoulder and thigh so severely that he was unable to work. I called on him to see how he was feeling. It was late morning and we were sitting in front of the cave, enjoying the sun which was shining for the first time after two or three days of rain and overcast skies. *Toiñito* was running around naked, barefooted and covered with the mud in which he was playing. Isabel, working in the cave, would have to scrub him before he could go inside.

As Antonio was telling me that he felt better and would soon be shining shoes again in the city of houses, he motioned to a *gitana* hurrying up the trail below the cave.

"Why is she in such a hurry?" he said.

"Who is she? Does she live near here?" I asked.

"It's Josefina, a cousin of Isabel. She lives *arriba*," which to Antonio meant anywhere above his cave.

When she drew nearer, I saw that she was a Gypsy in her late 30s. Under one arm, she was carrying a baby who seemed to be about two years old. An older boy, trying to keep up with the rapid pace, walked beside her.

On arriving at the cave, she threw a harassed look at us and asked, "Where is Isabel? I have to talk to her."

Antonio called Isabel.

The few seconds we waited for her gave me a chance to look at

Josefina and her children. She was a pretty *gitana*. Darker than Isabel, she was of medium height and slightly plump. Her older son, four years old, looked like Antonio's Joselito. He had a dark skin, black darting eyes and an intelligent face. The baby, whom she put down, was a beautiful boy, happy and active, with a lighter skin than the mother's.

As soon as Isabel came out of the cave, Josefina began to talk to her in an agitated manner. I heard references to *mercado*, a *paya*, *Dios* and *mal de ojo* (evil eye), but she spoke so rapidly I did not understand everything.

She remained for only a few minutes, and then continued her way along the trail above Antonio's cave toward her dwelling. I looked at Antonio, raising my eyebrows slightly to let him understand that I was interested in learning what had made her so excited.

"She said," Antonio told me with Isabel's listening, "that she is afraid her baby may have acquired *mal de ojo*." He went on to say that earlier in the morning in the Plaza de Abastos, where she was doing her daily shopping, a Castilian woman came up and put her face close to the baby's and exclaimed, "What a beautiful child!"

"That's right," said Isabel. "And Josefina feared the woman *ha echado mal de ojo* (had cast evil eye) onto the child."

To ward off the condition, Josefina told the woman to request God's blessing, "*Dios te bendiga*."

"Who gets evil eye?" I asked.

"Children about two years old," answered Isabel.

"And the more *jucal* (Caló for pretty) they are, the more likely they are to receive it," said Antonio.

Josefina's child filled both of these requirements.

"Is *mal de ojo* serious?"

"Yes, the baby can become very ill or even die from it," Antonio said.

"What are the symptoms?"

"The baby may vomit, have a fever, a headache, lose his appetite, and sometimes have eye trouble."

"What precautions does a mother take to give her child protection?"

Isabel answered, "Mothers try to keep their babies away from women who have the reputation of casting evil eye. The trouble is that some women who have the power do not realize that they have it. So when a mother is in public with her baby, she can never relax for fear of meeting one of these women. That is why Josefina was so upset. She feared that the *paya* had the power without realizing it."

"Don't forget amulets," Antonio said.

"Oh yes," said Isabel. "Josefina's baby had a pouch around his neck with hair from a badger."

Antonio added that, when they were small, his mother hung chestnuts around the necks of his brothers and sisters. He also said that grains of wheat, bread and salt, and an image of the Virgin are helpful. But I never saw any of these objects around the necks of Isabel's children.

I was in a different world. I had had a few hints of its existence — Concha's hurling a curse, and a Castilian youth who supposedly suffered paralysis from the curse of his girl friend's mother.

At breakfast the next morning I asked my interpreter of life among the poor, Miguel the waiter, what he thought about *mal de ojo*.

"Perhaps it exists," he said. "Everything is possible in life. Many people believe in it, my wife for one."

"Are there other beliefs like evil eye?"

"Many people believe in *antojos*. This has to do with the whims of a pregnant woman. If they are not satisfied, her baby may be marked or even be stillborn. A spot on the baby's skin could come from a flower the mother wanted but was denied."

When I went into the lobby after breakfast, Miguel called to the old laundry woman, all in black, who was passing by with an armful of sheets to be folded. "Tell the señor about your son who had evil eye."

"He almost died," she said. "He was going blind. I took him to la Señora Inés, a *curandera* who specialized in treating children with evil eye ailments. She cured him."

Jesús the hotel manager overheard our conversation. A skeptic, like many Andalusians, he laughed. "That's sheer superstition," he said. But the old lady did not recant.

In Fonelas I asked Camilo about village beliefs. "I don't believe in *mal de ojo*," he said. "Many villagers do, though. An old woman here is supposed to cast it. Another old woman can remove it." He continued, "I don't believe that the dead can come back to life, as some people do. A few years ago a Castilian villager claimed that he saw his deceased mother walking about the village. The priest held a Mass for her."

This conversation, and ones with other friends, showed me that not all Gypsies and poor Castilians believe in the supernatural world of which evil eye is one element. My skepticism was shared by others. I had no intention, though, of trying to change the beliefs of Antonio. At any rate, it was beyond my capability to do so. I was content to observe the evil eye drama as it unfolded, learning how it affected the lives of my *Guadijeño* friends and acquaintances.

It was a coincidence, but I found when talking about evil eye with Falcó and his wife, neither of whom believed in it, that it was Falcó's wife who had admired Josefina's child in the market. "I was surprised," she said, "when the *gitana* became upset. I had no idea that Gypsies feared Castilian women."

"It's all turned around now," said Falcó. "When I was a boy, it was the Castilians who were afraid of Gypsy women casting evil eye. It's not that way today."

"Oh yes it is!" said a city official, a daily visitor to the paper store. "My wife distrusts them, and when she walks our grandchild, she shields his face from Gypsy women."

But the old women, both in the city of Guadix and in the villages who were said to cast evil eye, were Castilians not Gypsies. The Gypsies themselves have long forgotten their Caló expression *querelar nasula* (throwing evil eye).

About ten days after Josefina had expressed fears about her baby, she told Isabel that he had a fever, a poor appetite and pains in his head. Isabel said that Josefina was taking him to Tía Francisca, a curer who treated the evil eye.

During the following weeks, I continued to seek out information. For example, I asked a schoolteacher in the Bar Molinillo what he knew about evil eye. "Not many people believe in it," he said.

"But I have talked with several *Guadijeños* who do. What about you?" I asked the bartender, who was listening.

"I don't, but my wife does. She puts things around the necks of our children, and she knows the *curanderos*."

A mailman acquaintance, who heard us talking about curers, said, "My wife and I use them. One is *el Tío Lástimas*." (the sad old man.)

"Do you know anyone whose child has had evil eye?"

He thought for a moment before replying. "Yes, it happened in my own family. When my boy was two, he became ill with a fever and an upset stomach. Someone had cast a spell onto him."

"Did you suspect who did it?"

"It was a drunken woman who lived in our neighborhood."

"What did you do?"

"We took her to *la Tía Francisca*. She rid the child of evil eye."

Here was another person who had taken his child to *Tía Francisca*. I wondered if I could talk to her. It might not be easily arranged, because curers were reluctant to discuss their healing techniques with strangers. I asked Antonio if he could arrange an interview.

"I used to shine the shoes of her husband," he said. "He had a small grocery store before he died. Do you want to see her now?"

When I told him I did, he finished his wine, put his shoe-shine gear in a corner of the bar where we were talking, and said, *"Nah-elamos!"* (Caló for "let's go".)

His swift response was typical of Gypsies, who liked to act rather than plan. This haste used to catch me unprepared in my early days in the region, but I soon came to enjoy the spontaneous events that they led to.

I asked Antonio how much Francisca charged for a visit.

"Nothing. Absolutely nothing."

This was unusual. Curers in northern Spain frequently charged fees, some becoming wealthy. But I found that Antonio was correct. None of the healers in the region charged for their curing.

We were now in the Magdalena quarter, once the center of Visigoth life in Guadix, and later the home of the *mozárabes* who retained their Christianity under the Moors. In a few minutes we came to my favorite church, La Magdalena, a baroque gem, but now abandoned and falling into ruins.

"She lives near here," Antonio said.

How fitting Francisca lived where, by tradition, the blood lines of the residents had remained intact for hundreds of years, from the Visigothic period through the occupation of the Moors, and from the Reconquest to the present day. It was even possible that she was a descendant of the Romans who had preceded the Visigoths, and who themselves believed in evil eye.

"I suppose," I said, "that Francisca has *gracia*," the quality I had been told all healers possessed. When he acknowledged that she did, I asked him what it meant.

"It comes from above, from a saint or the Virgin," he replied.

"How do you know when a person has grace?"

"All curers have it. Everyone knows that."

Soon we came upon three old Castilian ladies, dressed in black sitting in chairs at the edge of the street. Antonio spoke to one of them, a heavy-set woman in her seventies with gray hair combed straight back, wearing gold earrings.

"Francisca, can we talk to you? This foreigner wants to hear about your curing."

In a soft, pleasant voice, she said that she had no objections, and led us into her two-story house. Like the others in the quarter, it had its façade directly on the street, and a small patio with a circular garden in the middle. On the circumference, wooden pillars rose to support balconies which ran along the second floor. The house must have been built in the 1500s, about the same time as the Magdalena church.

We sat down in a small kitchen-living room, comfortably furnished and immaculately maintained. The walls were white and gleaming, and the tile floor was freshly scrubbed. This was the room where she received her patients.

Antonio, with Andalusian directness, said to me, "Go ahead. Ask some questions."

"How long have you been treating children for evil eye?" I asked.

"About forty years," Francisca replied.

"Do you treat broken bones, sprains, herpes, erysepeles and jaundice as some of the other curers do?"

"No, only evil eye."

I asked how she could tell that a child was ill from evil eye. She surprised me by stating that she did not attempt to identify the cause of the ailment, but accepted the diagnosis of the parents.

The subject of grace intrigued me, so I asked her if she had that quality.

"Yes," she said. "I do. It is a divine gift. Because of it, my treatments are successful."

"Can you tell me how you treat the symptoms?"

"I take the baby into another room, apart from the parents, and recite a secret prayer I learned from la Señora Inés. [This was the same *curandera* who had treated the son of the old laundry woman.] She treated my daughter for an evil eye condition. After the child was cured with the use of prayer, I asked Inés to reveal it to me. She agreed, but could do so only between midnight and eight in the morning on Good Friday. After waiting several months for Good Friday, I learned it."

"Do you also put drops of oil in water?" Antonio asked.

"No, I don't, but I know curers who do. If the oil disappears in the water, it means that a cure is possible."

Since I did not want to abuse her hospitality by asking too many questions, we didn't stay long. I'm not sure what kind of a person I had been expecting to see, but I was unprepared for the kindly old woman who had received us so hospitably. Regardless of how skeptics might view the concept of evil eye, it seemed that she was filling a need for those who believed in it. Later, though, I wondered if Francisca wasn't harming children by keeping them away from medical treatment. Perhaps she was, but many childhood ailments disappear whether treated or not. Also, all mothers were not like Josefina. Many did not believe in evil eye, and those who did, if noting no improvement in their children after treatment by a *curandera,* took them to a medical doctor.

Two weeks later while Antonio was shining my shoes in front of the Bar Dólar, he told me that Josefina's baby had died.

"Was it because of evil eye?" I asked.

He stopped wielding his brushes for a moment, and looked up at me gravely and nodded his head—and then went back to polishing my shoes.

Isabel, though, did not share his view, because when I asked her if she also felt that the child died from a condition of evil eye, she only looked at me with a quizzical expression. I remembered then that, when her children were ill, she took them to doctors in the government clinic, not to *curanderos.* Neither one cared to talk any more about it. It was probably just as well. What was to be gained from asking why *la Tía Francisca* hadn't cured the child? Antonio, who had the most faith in her healing powers, could easily have said that Josefina waited too long before taking the baby to see her. If I had asked why the family hadn't taken the child to a medical doctor, Antonio could have replied that doctors don't understand the evil eye.

Strangely enough, Josefina did not seek out and berate Falcó's wife for causing the death of her child. The couple were expecting that she would, and were prepared for an embarrassing incident, possibly Josefina's entering their store and publicly denouncing them.

Later, I learned that the origins of the belief in the evil eye, found among the residents of Spain and other Mediterranean countries—elsewhere, as well—is one of the world's mysteries. It is so strongly held that even though it leads to tragedy, as in the death of Josefina's child in Guadix, critics are unlikely to dislodge it.

# 12

# Lola, The Gypsy Virgin

And time, as you dance, is not,
and the world is as naught.
You dance, and I know the desire
of all flesh...

TO A GITANA DANCING (1899)
*Arthur Symons*

Lola was a fourteen year old *chaborí calé* (Gypsy girl), a cousin of Isabel. I first met her one spring evening in Antonio's cave when she and her mother, a full-bodied *gitana*, walked over for a visit from their cave-home in the next valley. I recognized her as one of four teen-age Gypsies who had already attracted my attention as they rapidly descended from the cave area to the city below, arms around one another, laughing and chatting. Because of their freshness and grace, I referred to them in my notes as "the fawns." In the city Lola and the other fawns wore brightly colored skirts and blouses, but here in the cave complex she had on a nondescript brownish dress, similar to what Isabel wore when doing her housework. Reaching only to her knees, it revealed her well-formed calves which, unlike the English and American Gypsies, she and the other *gitanas* of Guadix had no qualms about showing off.

When she smiled, her naturally red lips parted to reveal perfectly formed white teeth. She had a prominent Gypsy nose and high oriental cheek bones. Her bronze skin would have been the delight of the blonde Scandinavians I had seen lying in their bikinis in the hot Iberian sun along the Costa del Sol, striving to achieve the same metallic shade that Lola had come by naturally from her ancestors in the great Indian sub-continent.

She wore no make-up, but her eyebrows were as faint and delicate as though etched with a pencil. She was about five feet, five inches tall, and would probably be an inch or so taller before she stopped growing. Her figure, not yet fully formed, was slender but strong. One day, she would fill out to be like her mother, robust—not fat. Her hair was long and black, and fell to her shoulders after being caught in the back of her head by a small yellow ribbon which was her only decoration. She wore no rings, bracelets or earrings. These would come with marriage.

I avoided staring at Lola, and rarely spoke to her directly. Because the Gypsies saw me as an unattached male, they would take affront if I paid too much attention to her. But I tried to make every glance count to store up details of her appearance in the event that I did not see her close-up again. I had no way of knowing at that time that I would one day see her perform a primitive, almost pre flamenco dance. What impressed me most about her at that first meeting was the air of latent wildness about her person. The haughty tossing of her head, and her penetrating stare made the onlooker aware that she was the descendant of a people who had successfully held onto their proud spirit despite their thousand years of wandering.

Lola and her mother stayed for only a few minutes, and then left for their cave. In the time they were in Antonio's home, they had quickly glanced in my direction, but had said nothing to me, following Gypsy etiquette of not speaking to strangers unless the husband or father were present.

After they were gone, Antonio said in the low, confidential tone he used when about to reveal something related to Gypsy lore, *"Ella es rúa."* (She is a virgin.) Antonio's vocabulary in Caló was small, so I was surprised that he knew *rúa*, another of the words carried out of India.

"And another thing," he added, "She cannot *querrar* until she marries."

Antonio had used *querrar*, because of the confidentiality of the conversation. Its original meaning in Caló was "to make" or "to do." Among the Gypsies of Guadix, it had come to mean "to make physical love."

I was flattered that Antonio had brought up such a sensitive subject, but he did not have to tell me that Lola was (or most likely was) a virgin. I had assumed she was from what I had already heard about the *chaborís* retaining their virginity. Falcó in the city below, although despising the Gypsies, was quick to grant them this virtue. And writers on the Spanish Gypsies have often commented on it. Cervantes has Preciosa in *The Little Gypsy Girl* deliver a long declaration on her sexual morals:

Only one jewel I possess, and to me it is
worth more than life itself; that jewel is
my integrity and virginity, and I shall not
sell it in exchange for promises or gifts...
You shall have it only if wrapped in the
bonds of marriage...

From what I saw in the weeks that followed, Lola's conduct conformed to the behavior expected of teen-agers. She didn't smoke or drink alcoholic beverages and didn't go about alone. Whenever she came to Antonio's cave, either her mother or a brother or sister was with her. Lola would not indulge in the pre-marital liaisons permitted by some other societies. Unlike Castilian girls, she would not stroll through the cave area or in the city streets arm-in-arm with her *novio* (boyfriend or fiance). There would be no engagement period. The first time she was with a boy alone, she must marry him. She did not lead a secluded life, though. She visited friends and relatives in the cave complex, and frequently went into the city.

Castilians were well aware of the code governing the conduct of Gypsy girls. No boys or young men would dare to whistle at Lola, and no one would call after her as they might after a Castilian girl: *"Bendita la madre que te parió!"* (Bless the mother who brought you into the world!) or other *piropos* (flowerly complements.) I doubt that Lola carried a knife, although some *gitanas* did, but what the following flamenco stanza says about another Lola also applied to the Lola of Guadix:

*No te metas con La Lola.*
*Su familia tiene cuchillos*
*pa defender su persona.*
 Don't bother Lola.
 Her family has knives
 To defend her with.

Because of the Gypsy restraints, I wondered how Lola would go about selecting a boy to marry. To the outsider, the system seemed to be awkward, but to Lola, who had grown up within its framework, it presented no difficulties.

"She knows the boys she played with as a little girl," said Antonio. "She sees boys when they are walking by. Her girl friends tell her about boys who like her, and so do her parents. And, you know, she might marry a boy from Granada or from a village."

I saw a brief meeting between *chaborós* and *chaborís* one Saturday when Lola and the fawns came whirling into the open-air market. Shortly after they arrived, they met a group of *chaborós*. The meeting lasted only a few seconds, but it was long enough for the *churumbeles* (young people) to stand next to each other and to exchange a few words. Lola was excited as the others and, from where I stood, I could hear her laughter. Then it was over. The girls whirled in one direction, the boys in another. Because the boys were so well dressed, I had a feeling that the encounter was prearranged.

Lola's virginity, though, had nothing to do with prudery as I found out one evening in Antonio's cave when she was present while I was reviewing some words in Caló with Antonio and Isabel. They included intimate parts of the body: *cará* for vagina, *magué* for penis and *anrés* for testicles. As each one was pronounced, Lola nodded, showing that she knew its meaning.

The Gypsy custom of the *chaborí* retaining her virginity exists in other countries as well as in Spain. After a girl has been observed with a boy alone in the United States and England, proof sometimes has to be established that she has not lost her virginity. An older woman, or even a medical doctor, may physically examine her. In early 1978, in the Court of Appeals in Washington, D.C., a Gypsy family, in the absence of a birth certificate, based its contention that an unmarried daughter was a juvenile when she was arrested for burglary on the grounds that she was a virgin, and Gypsy women remained virgins until they are eighteen.

"Antonio," I asked, "whom will she marry?"

"I don't know, but it will have to be a Gypsy."

He was reinforcing what I already knew. The Gypsies realize that to remain Gypsies they must marry other Gypsies. (The village priest in Benalúa, which has the largest concentration of Gypsies in the region, told me that during his twenty years in the village he had not married a Gypsy to a non-Gypsy.) Cervantes, who harbored a good bit of skepticism about Gypsy life, had another view of their insistence on intramarriage. In the *Dogs' Colloquy* he wrote, "They always marry among themselves, so that their evil ways don't come to the notice of the outside world."

But if Gypsies marry only other Gypsies, what about the fair ones — and red-headed ones? What is their origin? How do the Gypsies themselves account for them, if *gitanas* are loyal to husbands?

Antonio faced up to these questions realistically. He knew that if color of skin were one of the principal criteria for determining that a person was a Gypsy, he would be disqualified because of his light olive complexion. One day when we were on this subject, a delicate one for me to discuss with a Gypsy, he pointed out his skin, saying, "We are not all dark. Through the years things have happened between men and women. But I am a Gypsy. I have *arati*." (Gypsy blood)

In the several weeks that followed my first meeting with Lola, I continued to see her, sometimes in Antonio's cave and sometimes in the city below. One day, I had an unusual view of her while I was sitting in the sun on top of Cerro de la Bala. Looking down over the edge, I saw Lola and a younger sister begin to climb up one of the steep ridges on the flank of the peak. They were looking for a small brother who, along with other children of the cave city, liked to play on the summit plateau. Lola was climbing in her bare feet. Although the route was covered with loose stones, she moved easily and showed no fear of falling, as she called down encouragement to her sister below. Her graceful mastery of the precipitous arête reminded me of the *gitana* in Seville whom George Borrow described in the 1830s as appearing to soar like a falcon.

On a cool evening later that summer, several of us were sipping wine while sitting on low, cane stools around a wood fire outside Antonio's cave. Neighbors drifted in and out of the circle, but the nucleus was Antonio and his wife; Luis, Antonio's eighteen year old brother; Black Beret and his wife, and myself. We were listening to Antonio's flamenco records played on a battered record player. Luis was casually plucking the strings of a guitar. He seemed to have a natural feel for the instrument. He had been playing regularly for only a year or so, but was already better than most of the other local Gypsies.

After awhile, from out of the dusk, Lola and her mother came to join us.

"*Quiere bailar?*" (Want to dance?) Antonio asked, looking at Lola.

She was willing, and after glancing at her mother for approval, cast off her cloth sandals and stood quietly in her bare feet for a few minutes by the fire. How different she was from the Gypsies at the commercial flamenco performances at Granada's Sacromonte. The *gitanas* there wore heavy make-up with false eyelashes. Their stage costume was the *traje de gitano*, long polka-dot, flouncy dresses, cut low to a "V" between the breasts, and high-heeled shoes. Lola's costume was a well-worn, brown skirt and a white, sleeveless blouse that was too small. Her face showed no trace of rouge or lipstick; her fingernails were free of polish. She had no tambourine or castanets.

She placed her hands firmly on her hips, arched her back and threw her head back, showing the firm lines of her youthful neck. To give her more room to dance, we pushed our chairs back, and, as Luis increased the tempo of his playing, she began to dance slowly while we encouraged her with our cries.

"*Olé! Olé!*"

"*Así se baila!*" (That's the way to dance!)

"*Anda! Anda!*" (Go! Go!)

She increased the speed of her dancing, bare arms held above her head, bent at the elbows and wrists. She snapped her fingers for a few moments, and then extended them in flamenco style with forefingers and thumbs stretched to the fullest, the other fingers bent so that the little finger stood out by itself. Her footwork was natural and fluid, and her arms moved gracefully.

She had never seen a professional performance, and was probably better off for it. Hers was no fixed routine. She danced only when she felt like it, improvising as she went along.

She suddenly stopped, and sat by her mother on one of the stools. She needed a rest, and also wanted to observe the reaction of her audience. We responded as one, clapping our hands and again shouting, "*Ole! Ole!*" This show of appreciation was her only reward for the entertainment she was providing us.

I hadn't expected her to dance. It was my good fortune to be there for a real Gypsy dance. Flamenco is not performed commercially in Guadix. Though there are too few tourists to make it commercially feasible, the main reason is the shopkeeper's dislike of flamenco. A merchant in Falcó's shop referred to it contemptuously, saying, "Folklore music doesn't exist here," and, "It does nothing to us to hear a Gypsy break his voice when he sings." As a result, flamenco occurs only among the caves for the Gypsies' own enjoyment —and there it is impromptu as was Lola's dance that evening.

After a few minutes she was ready to begin again. Luis vigorously struck several chords, and the rest of us began our *jaleo* (rhythmic accompaniment). We had all improved. I was doing better with my *palmas* (hand-clapping), and was also producing some acceptable tongue clacking. Antonio's *pitos* (finger-snapping) were more definitive. Our *zapateado* (foot-stamping) didn't resound from the earth the way it would have from a wooden floor, but Lola could still hear it. Members of a flamenco group in Granada's Sacromonte would have scoffed at our clumsiness. But we were enjoying ourselves and had no need for castanets or black suits with short coats to support our efforts.

To my surprise, Black Beret—I had no idea he could sing—burst into snatches of song, breaking his voice in Gypsy style, hoarsely shouting verses that I could not understand. His wife, shyly smiled her approval, and Antonio supported him with a cry of, "That's the way to sing!"

Luis started to play a *fandango* from La Peza, a hill town in the region, and Black Beret sang the words to it:

I am from La Peza, pezeño
From the mountain, mountaineer,
And to serve you
I am from Granada, Granadino.

Lola stood up, a Gypsy princess continuing an ancient tradition of her race. Her right arm was above her head; her left arm rested on her hip supported by the back of her wrist. This time, the dance was wilder and more abandoned. When she held both arms outstretched, her short blouse rose to expose the taut skin of her midriff, and when she whirled, her skirts flew above her knees exposing firm, bronze thighs. Her dance was filled with passion, and I felt a sensuousness emanating from her body.

Was she the Gypsy girl I had dreamt about as a boy? Because, despite my mother's implanting the fear of the Gypsies in me with her tales of kidnapping, I had heard about the pretty, brown-skinned Gypsy girls who sold baskets from door to door, and had imagined their sensuality. Was she the flamenco dancer I had fancied embracing as a young man? Perhaps...but then I remembered Borrow, who had written that no females in the world can be more licentious in word and gesture, in dance and song, had quickly added that a gleaming knife awaited anyone who tried to take advantage of them. And so it was with this passionate *chaborí*. No one would clasp her in his arms except during elopement and marriage.

Between steps she came to abrupt halts, breaking the flow of move-ment, her body held immobile, injecting suspense into her per-formance, and also permitting her to gather strength before continuing.

As I watched her spin around the fire, her long hair flying, she seemed to my imagination to be a descendant of the pre-Roman Celto-Iberians who, according to Strabo, the Greek geographer, lived here along the river Guadix (then the river Dourios) and danced in front of their dwellings until dawn.

A daydream, of course, because Lola's ancestors didn't arrive in Spain until fourteen hundred years after Strabo. But I still like to think of Lola as carrying on a tradition ante-dating the Christian era, a tradition perhaps rediscovered in the 1400s when the Gypsies met indigenous peoples in the caves of Andalusia who still remembered the Celtic dances.

With the support of Luis' guitar and our *jaleo*, Lola had achieved a state of *duende*, lost in the flow of the dance rhythm, unmindful of her surroundings. Her arms, held in front of her body, were bent at the elbows with her fingers extended in a position of supplication. Her eyes were closed, and on her face was an expression of ecstasy. The climax of the dance had been reached. It lasted for only a few seconds, but in that brief period we experienced a oneness with Lola and her primitive dance.

In the late fall of that year, Antonio said to me, "It is time that Lola marries. She is fifteen. She is taller and her *cuchas* (breasts) are fuller. She is ripe. Most of the girls her age are already married. Some are mothers."

Her brief time as a teenager was about to close. She had no regrets. This was her way of life, and she wanted no other but to marry, have children, and, in so doing, perpetuate the Gypsy race. By the time she was seventeen, she would have at least one child, but during her married life, she probably would not have the twelve that her mother did. *Gitanas* of her generation were having fewer children.

I was certain that by now one of the several handsome *chaborós* in the cave complex, who had spoken to her in the park, or had watched her dance by the light of the campfire, had somehow been able to sing a love song within her hearing:

*Chaborí! Con tu*
*fresca mui roja*
*negras sacais dañosas*
*dañí de nacar*
*tú sinlas jucal*
*abiya con mangué.*

> Gypsy girl! With your
> Fresh red mouth
> Black mischievous eyes
> Teeth of mother-of-pearl
> You are lovely
> Come with me.

One night Isabel said that Lola had decided on her *novio*. He was an outgoing sixteen-year-old bootblack named Pepe whose family lived in a cave near Lola's. Within a few weeks he eloped with Lola to Granada where they spent several days. Their elopement, known as *va a llevarse la novia*, was a happy combination of Gypsy and Castilian traditions in Andalusia. Among Gypsies it is a reminder of the time when brides were actually kidnapped, and among Castilians it is an established tradition that continues to the present day.

Upon returning to Guadix, Lola and Pepe, happy young lovers, received no criticisms from the other Gypsies because of their intimacy before marriage. They moved into her parents' cave where they would live until acquiring their own dwelling. A few days after their return, they were married in church, a contrast to the practice of a generation ago when many Gypsy couples lived together without ever getting married. This doesn't mean that Gypsies are becoming more religious. A church marriage provides documentation for social security benefits.

At the wedding celebration, there was no *pañuelo* (handkerchief), or *diklo* as it is known in Caló, the custom providing proof that the *gitana* was a virgin until the day of her marriage. Juan de Dios Ramirez, the Gyspy author, who approves of the three principles which should govern a *gitana's* life as virginity, marriage and perpetuation of the species, refers to the *diklo* as a ritual. He calls it the moment of discovering truth. He then expresses his displeasure with Gypsiologists who through the years have betrayed this ceremony in their articles and books.

Antonio had no compunctions about discussing *diklo*. In explaining it to me he said, "A friend of the bride's family, usually an old lady, enters the bridal chamber, returning with a handkerchief spotted with blood, which she then shows to the family of the groom. The custom is dying out, though, as more young Gypsies elope before marriage."

But even if the practice disappears altogether, it will continue to exist in memory and in song. Several popular flamenco verses refer to it. One of them goes like this:

> In a green meadow
> I stretched out my kerchief.
> Three roses appeared
> Like morning stars.

If there were no *pañuelo* for Lola and her husband, they did keep another Gypsy tradition. It was the custom of having a baby as soon as possible. A few months after the wedding, Isabel told me that Lola was *cambrí* (pregnant), and early the following summer, she gave birth to a bronze baby girl who, within a few years, would be dancing the wild flamenco in front of her cave as had her mother—and Strabo's Celto-Iberians.

# 13

# Undebel and Ben
## (God and Devil)

They conform to the Catholic religion
but are looked upon as unbelievers.

TRAVELS THROUGH SPAIN
IN THE YEARS 1775 AND 1776

*Henry Swinburne*

One Sunday morning in May, I went to Mass in the cathedral with two friends. On leaving its dim interior, it took me several seconds to become accustomed to the harsh Andalusian light. Castaño the guide whizzed past me on his motorcycle in hot pursuit of a German tourist. Then I saw Antonio shining the shoes of a man at the foot of the steps leading down to the plaza. He gave no sign that he had seen me as we strolled past to cross the plaza for some *grifos* (draft beer) in the Bar Cazadores (Bar of the Hunters) with its deer heads—and photographs of Franco—on the walls. But Antonio was adept at pretending not to see people, and I thought it likely he had noticed me.

I was right. An hour or so later when I met him in front of the Bar Dólar, where he was sitting on his shoe-shine box, he looked me squarely in the face, and without even a *"Buenas tardes. Cómo está?"* asked, "Do you believe?" His question would have embarrassed me when I first arrived in Guadix, but I had become accustomed to Gypsies and the poor Castilians asking about my personal affairs. My rule-of-thumb was to reply truthfully, although sometimes a polite, noncommital answer sufficed.

Aside from the feeling of tranquility it gave me to be honest with friends and acquaintances, there was another advantage. After a straightforward response, it was my turn to ask questions of the questioner who, according to the custom of Andalusia, was usually willing to respond in the same way. So when Antonio queried me on the sidewalk in front of the bar, I answered him honestly.

128

It was too complex a subject, though, to respond with a simple "*sí*" or "*no*." Yet, I didn't want to give a complicated answer, because his knowledge of formal religion was limited. He was aware of the existence of Protestants, because there were Jehovahs Witnesses or *Testigos de Yehová* in the city, but I did not want to become enmeshed in the nuances of Protestantism. So while he was shining my shoes, I began with "I believe in some things, but not in everything."

This was too vague for Antonio. "Do you believe in the Virgin?" He had heard that Protestants reduced the importance of Mary in their worship.

"Antonio, that's a rough question," I said, not wanting to discuss Mary's position in Christianity.

But this, along with my previous response, was too indefinite from Antonio's view to account for my attending Mass. So he came out with another direct question, "Then, why do you go to Mass?"

Although I had to answer his question almost immediately, I still had time to laugh to myself over the humor of the situation. I was being interrogated about my religious beliefs—a modern-day Inquisition—by a Gypsy bookblack. But I answered Antonio seriously. "I enjoy the music and the peacefulness in the cathedral. It gives me a chance to relax and think."

This seemed to satisfy him. It was now my turn to ask questions about his beliefs, and using his technique of the short, direct question, I asked, "Do you believe?"

"I believe. I believe in *el Señor* (Jesus) and the Virgin. And my children are baptized." He quickly added, "But we don't go to Mass."

"Why not?" I asked.

"Because we Gypsies don't like to," he replied.

This was the same answer he had given me when I had asked him why Gypsies did not take part in the *paseo*, the evening stroll through the park. The *paseo*, it had seemed to me, was too formal for the Gypsies. Mass, with its emphasis on ritual, would be even more so.

By then, he had finished shining my shoes, so I said, "Antonio, we have been in the sun long enough. Let's go inside for a drink."

He was agreeable and followed me into the bar which was one of the bars that did not welcome Gypsies, except its resident Gypsy, el Golondrina. Because he was with me, Antonio was acceptable.

In the coolness of the bar, I thought about our discussion. My earlier visits to his cave had confirmed his attachment (and Isabel's) to the

Virgin and Christ. The cave walls were hung with their images—similar to those in the caves of other Gypsies and non-Gypsies, as well. And as for the Gypsies not going to Mass, my observations bore out Antonio's remarks. That morning in the cathedral, there had been no Gypsies, and few of the city's other poor. And few Gypsies attended Mass in the two churches in the city of caves.

"We don't wear religious medals," Antonio said.

I hadn't thought about it, but after that as I looked at Gypsies in the city, I saw that none wore medals, although many non-Gypsies did.

"What about Holy Days?" I asked.

"Sometimes we watch the processions, but we don't march in them, and we don't carry saints."

This didn't surprise me. There are Gypsies elsewhere in Spain who help to carry images of the saints, but I could not picture the Gypsies of Guadix so engaged.

Later, on Corpus Christi day, I noted that it was the shopkeepers and their families who strolled arm-in-arm watching the parade in which the statue of Christ was born by a religious fraternity of businessmen. Only one or two of my friends from Ramón de la Toñica were there. Neither was Falcó—he and his wife seldom attended these events. To my surprise, though, I saw Antonio and his children in front of the cathedral along with a handful of other Gypsies.

Antonio and Isabel enjoyed the fiesta at the Ermita de Fátima on the edge of the cave city. It was a day filled with so many activities (two Masses, a procession, bicycle race and fireworks) that a program of events was distributed. One year during the festival I went into the Ermita during the Mass with Antonio and another Gypsy, who had just returned from Perpignan in France after a month of picking apricots. The church was filled with cave dwellers, but except for Antonio and his friend, the only other Gypsies were a *gitana* and her two children.

After a few minutes, his friend nudged me, shaking his head to indicate his disinterest, and left. Antonio soon became restless. "*Vámanos!*" he said, and I went out with him. We spoke to some other Gypsies who were outside drinking beer and soda pop. They were waiting for the procession, which would begin at the conclusion of the Mass. A band from the village of Alquife was warming up its instruments, and a driver of a John Deere tractor was maneuvering it into position at the entrance of the church to pull a wagon with an image of the Virgin of Fátima mounted on it during the procession.

I wondered how the priests felt about the faith of the Gypsies, and decided to talk to several of them. Would I get a reaction similar to what George Borrow received in Córdoba? There an old priest warned him that those of the Egyptian faith were evil. Borrow came to accept this view. He felt that the secret monitor which governs mens' actions was weakly rooted among the Gypsies. The priests of Guadix shared this attitude.

The first one I interviewed was apparently under the impression that I was seeking to gain adherents to Protestantism — he had a reputation for being very conservative. He quickly said, "The Gypsies are all Catholics," and he repeated, *"Todos, todos son católicos."* He added that they receive final sacraments. But he then went on to express his doubts about them. "They are stubborn, hard, unmalleable, and lazy."

Another priest, who was an official in the Bishop's palace, confirmed Antonio's earlier remarks. *"Los cumplimientos — nada."* (Sunday obligations — none.) "And," he added, "not even on Easter." Juan Sánchez, a priest in Granada, author of *Granada y sus gitanos*, said to me, "They are Catholic in name only." A university student said, "What disturbs the priests most is their failure, after centuries of persuasion, to convince the Gypsies that they should attend Mass."

It seemed to me, though, that the priests misunderstood Antonio and the other Gypsies. None of the ones I knew criticized the church and none laughed at images of Christ on the Cross, as did some of my atheist Castilian acquaintances. Antonio's beliefs were similar in some ways to those of a businessman friend in the city who never went to Mass, and who derided priests and nuns. Nonetheless, he held sacred the Virgin of Carmen and stopped at a roadside shrine, dedicated to her, to offer up his prayers. Antonio stopped at no roadside chapel, but in his own way he worshipped *the* Virgin, the one whose image was in his cave.

Antonio didn't know it, but his ancestors had embraced several different faiths on their long trail through the Near East to Spain before becoming Roman Catholics. As they became exposed to the religions of the various countries they passed through, they gradually forgot their original beliefs and acquired new ones. Those who remained in the Near East became Moslems; those who crossed into Greece became Greek Orthodox — and the ones who continued into Western Europe became Roman Catholic and Protestant.

"Don't forget," said a friend, "Being Catholic in Spain helped them escape the Inquisition, although their poverty was also a factor — they had none of the riches and property of the Jews and Moors to confiscate. A Spanish saying, popular during the Inquisition, aptly described their economic position, '*Más pobre que cuerpo de gitano.*' " (Poorer than the body of a Gypsy.)

Late one afternoon, I happened to meet Antonio on the Cruz de Piedra. I invited him for a drink along with a Gypsy named Ramòn, who had been working in Barcelona for a year. We turned onto the Road of the Strangers and entered a large bar. On the walls were large pin-ups of scantily-clad women. (This was during the closing years of the Franco regime, and censorship was becoming less restrictive.) The bartender put a plate of raw lima beans in their pods in front of us.

"Do you like beans?" asked Ramón as he shelled a handful, dropping the empty pods onto the floor. *Bobís* was Caló for beans, a word familiar to many *guadijeños*, as well as to Gypsies. I told him that I did, shelling my own, and popping them into my mouth without removing the thin covering on the bean itself which Antonio was doing. From eating them in bars that May—they are a spring crop in Guadix— I had learned to like them without taking this extra step.

Ramón had served in the Spanish Army for three years in the Sahara and showed me a photo of himself in uniform. After chatting briefly about his military experiences, I asked him if he knew any Caló.

"Only a little," he replied. "Words like *jundunaré, pañí, rom, chaboró* and *chaborí.*"

Antonio and I began to add to his meager vocabulary with some other commonly known words. The session was going smoothly until I asked, "Do you know the meaning of *undebel* (God) and *ben* (devil)?"

Antonio became upset, and frowned at me, shaking his head to indicate that I should not continue. I asked him why he objected. He answered in a low voice, "I don't want the Castilian bartender and some of these other non-Gypsies standing near us to know these words."

I changed the subject. Ramón, however, did not share Antonio's feelings, and looked at me with a half smile to indicate his skepticism.

On the surface, Antonio's position was not logical. I knew several Castilians from the city of caves whose Caló vocabulary exceeded Antonio's meager one. But Antonio's reaction wasn't based on logic; it came from an instinctive feeling that, even though there were no special powers associated with these terms, to share their meaning with *payos* would reveal secrets that should be kept from them. To

Antonio, it would make the Gypsies less Gypsy. No matter to him that books have been written about Romany Caló. Antonio did not know about them. No matter to him that I knew Caló—he regarded me as an exception because I was so close to him and other Gypsies. He did not know (and would not have cared to know) that *undebel* and *ben* are both Indic related.

Antonio knew other Caló words related to religion: *cangrí* (church) and *errajaí* (priest). But he did not value them as highly as *undebel* and *ben*. He did not know *majarí* for Virgin, or *peniche* (Holy Spirit). I never stopped marvelling that Antonio and the other Gypsies still knew these words. Linguists had told me they doubted an illiterate people like the Gypsies, away from their homeland for hundreds of years, could hold onto their own terms for the supernatural. Such words are supposed to be replaced by ones from the religions of the countries in which they have lived.

Of what use, I wondered, were words like *undebel* and *ben* to Antonio and the other Gypsies? Why did a poor Gypsy bootblack, who could neither read nor write, still know Sanskrit-derived words for God and devil when he had satisfactory ones in the Spanish *Dios* and *diablo*? He had no use for them in the practice of secret rites which, though Gypsies have long been suspected of nurturing them, did not exist in the region of Guadix. And it is unlikely that Antonio's ancestors, on their entry into Spain in the 1400s, remembered more than a few fragments of the faith from their Indian heritage.

In the 1830s, Borrow found no survivals of Indian beliefs, and neither did Alexandros Paspates in the 1870s in Turkey and Greece. Today, the only remnant in Europe of their early beliefs is in southeastern Macedonia, where on St. George's day the Gypsies celebrate a legend of the Hindu God Indra. The lack of a religion of their own makes it all the more extraordinary that Antonio and his ancestors have remained Gypsies during their long residence in the West. Unlike the Jews, with whom they are sometimes compared because of their wandering and persecutions, they have not had a traditional faith to support them in remaining a people apart.

All that was left of the Hindu-related beliefs, carried by his ancestors out of the great Indian subcontinent, was a mere handful of words: *Undebel, ben, majarí* and *errajaí*. Antonio did not look on *undebel* and *ben* as substitutes for *Dios* and *diablo*. They were a slender tie to the distant past, a past so dimly  remembered that even his ancestral  home was forgotten.

# 14

# An Off-Color Poem
# And Hunting Snails

My first snail-hunting expedition was the result of a bluntly-worded poem in Caló about making love.

It all began at about ten o'clock on a hot Saturday morning. I was on my way to the mercado del sábado after having visited Falcó in his store. It wasn't a simple matter to get there. At the Plaza de Abastos I met Pepe el Pando, my drinking companion from the tavern of Ramón, who had left his wife to tend their vegetable-fruit stand while he had a glass of brandy across the street in the Bar Calatrava on Juan de Austria Street where market workers gathered. I joined him for two drinks—he bought the first and I the second.

On leaving him, I met two strange *gitanas* who pestered me for money for, they said, a sick relative. "It's the Gypsies who have all the *trejulas* (money)," I told them. My statement didn't sound convincing until a familiar-sounding male voice from in back of me called out, "*Chachipé!*" It was el Golondrina. While passing by, he had sized up the situation and come to my support. Continuing on my way along the busy Almería road, I stopped briefly to chat with two Gypsy smiths, Carlos and Ramón, who were displaying their wares on the sidewalk. As I approached the Bar Molinillo next to the park, blind Rodrigo and Rosario came along selling lottery tickets. We went into the bar, crowded with Saturday clients, so that I could get change to buy some tickets. After a glass of wine together, they left.

Two middle-aged friends from the cave-dwelling village of Fonelas then came in. One of them, Pepe del Bigote, was part Gypsy and part

134

Castilian. He had a black, drooping mustache. The other was a Gypsy—lithe, bronze Manuel. Local Gypsies were not welcome in this bar, but presentable out-of-town ones, especially if with a Castilian, were accepted.

"*Tapiyamos mol?*" (Want to drink some wine?) I asked.

They both laughed and ordered a glass of *tinto* (red wine). The reason they were amused was that the previous year they had taught these words to me. Pepe had learned Caló as a boy growing up among the Gypsies. Along with Manuel, he knew more of the langauge than most Gypsies. After chatting for a few minutes, they said they would write me a poem in Caló. Borrowing a pencil, they put their heads together, and using the bar as a table top, laboriously jotted down the following verse:

*El jillar de una barim*
*sin bueno para un calé.*
*se le chinela con el cal*
*abela un chaboró.*

The vagina of a Gypsy bride
is good for the Gypsy husband.
Filled with his penis
From it comes a baby.

The poem isn't just in Caló. It is a combination of Caló and Spanish. What remains of the Romany language that the Gypsies carried with them into Spain is now a few hundred words with Spanish grammar and, usually, Spanish verb endings. The poem is interesting because so many of the words are Caló: *Jillar, barim, sin, calé, chinela, cal, abela* and *chaboró.* I found it had long been popular among the Gypsies. A retired Castilian school teacher gave me almost the same version. He had received it from a Gypsy over fifty years ago.

When I was asking Pepe and Manuel questions about the Caló between mouthfuls of a hot fish *tapa*, Antonio the bootblack entered the bar with his shoe-shine equipment seeking clients. Overhearing some of the words I was using, he became furious. Unable to control his emotions, he grabbed me by the arm. "I have something to show you," he said, while pulling me out of the bar to my embarrassment and to the astonishment of the others.

As soon as we were outside, he exploded, "These words are insulting! Throw them away! They are bad!" He continued, "Haven't I shown you much about Gypsy life? Trust me! Those others (he didn't know them) are trying to make a fool of you."

I was so taken aback that I could think of nothing to say—or to do. It was a perplexing situation. I couldn't let myself be angry with Antonio, even though he had embarrassed me in front of Manuel and Pepe, so I stood quietly with him in front of the bar. To underline his objections, he added forcefully, "I am more Gypsy than they are!"

Again, I was quiet. What he said was true for Pepe del Bigote, who wasn't entirely Gypsy, but Manuel with his dark skin, strong nose and piercing black eyes looked to be more Gypsy than Antonio. To be sure, Antonio wasn't talking about exterior appearances, but about what a Gypsy thinks about himself, deep down inside. And, even there, Manuel was as proud of being a Gypsy as was Antonio.

Antonio led me to a small bar, the Bar Appolo, in back of el Molinillo. Still grumbling about the episode, he bought me a brandy. "Two strong ones," he said to the woman who owned the bar.

When we were getting acquainted, Antonio had introduced me to the Guadix custom of drinking brandy in the morning. He started the day off with brandy, eating no breakfast at all, and had another one at mid-morning. It was a custom for which I never acquired a liking.

Antonio gulped his down—and I gulped mine down. "Two more," he said, and when the woman poured them he asked for water to wash them down. With or without water, it tasted just as vile to me.

Because Antonio was more relaxed, I asked, "What was it you didn't like about the poem?"

"*Jillar* and *cal*," he replied. "It is not good to use them in public in front of *payos*."

His reaction was similar to what it was in the bar some time before when I was explaining the meaning of *undebel* and *ben* to the Gypsy who did not know their meaning. With only other Gypsies present, the words could be used, but they were not for *payos* to overhear. In the privacy of his cave, the "off-color" words were acceptable, even in front of female members of the family. When I read a list of words in Caló to him, his wife, and mother-in-law to see how many words they knew, at first I omitted words such as *jinar* (to defecate), *mutrar* (to urinate) and *bul* (anus) that they might find objectionable. But as I introduced these words into the conversation, I found that they recognized them and were at ease with them.

Antonio announced that he was hungry. (He was still trying to think of what he was going to show me.) So we walked to a booth a few feet away where a man and his wife made *churros*. They are too heavy and I dislike them, but I ate one to keep Antonio company. While we were eating, Antonio asked, "Do you want to see some *caracoles* (snails)?"

I thought he meant we would visit someone who was selling them, as Gypsies frequently did at the market. So I replied, "Why not?"

Antonio left his shoe-shine gear with the owner of the small bar where we had drunk the brandy, and beckoned for me to follow him. We dropped into the dry bed of the River Guadix, which is about fifty yards wide here, and began to walk to the other side. The bed is used, as it has been through the centuries, as a roadway for work animals to and from Guadix.

When Antonio stopped at the far bank to pick up a few stray plastic sacks left by travellers along the river route, I realized that we were not going to look at snails in someone's basket. We were going to seek them ourselves. Poor Antonio! When we left the Bar Molinillo, he had no idea of what we were going to do. Hunting snails meant that he would miss the most lucrative day in the week for his shoe-shine business. The city on Saturday was full of potential clients. When he returned to his cave that day, he would have little money for Isabel to do her shopping with.

Falcó, to whom I described the incident, said, "You see, they are all lazy. He could have returned to his work. And what right did this Gypsy have to interfere in the conversation with your friends. *Ay!* These Gypsies!"

It seemed to me, though, that Antonio's putting away his shoe-shine gear was more a reflection of what another friend had said, "They don't worry about the future the way we do." Swept away by his feelings, Antonio was not concerned with making money. His concern was with my exposure to Caló words he considered to be taboo.

I welcomed the chance to pick snails for the first time. Also, walking in the sun would get rid of some of the alcohol I had stored in my system that morning.

We started up a narrow, dirt lane leading toward cultivated land of vegetables and fruit trees.

"Where does this road go?" I asked.

"It's the old road to Baza, but we follow it for only a short distance."

On our left was the chapel of San Sebastián, now abandoned, where once travellers leaving the city prayed for a safe trip. Someone had scrawled on the wall nearest us, *"Si Dios existe, es su problema."* (If God exists, it is his problem.)  Guadix was on the Republican side during the Civil War, and there were still many free-thinkers among its residents.

Higher up, the snow-capped Sierra beyond Guadix came into sight. As had the Moors, I loved this view of the city, and never tired of it. Carlos Asenjo the historian told me that this was the view over which the vanguard of the conquering army of Ferdinand and Isabella had marvelled when negotiating for the surrender of the city.

Antonio was quiet. He had talked himself out. I was thinking about the words in the poem that had disturbed him. They weren't the only ones of a similar nature in the Caló of Guadix. Besides *jillar*, there were two other words for female genitals: *cara* and *jojoi*, which also means rabbit. In addition to *cal* for male genitals, there was *magué*, and also *anrés* for testicles. The Guadix Caló had three expressions for making love: *rilar*, *bandar* and *querar*. I wondered if all dying languages had so many similar terms.

Continuing along the lane, which was lined with olive and almond trees, we soon gained enough altitude to enjoy a view of Guadix with the sun shining on the sparkling white fronts of the caves in the hills above the brown Moorish fortress. We passed a few poor farm houses, and came upon a man in rubber boots irrigating fields of corn and sugar beets. The fields were terraced and the banks separating one from the other were about two and a half feet high. Pointing toward one of these banks, Antonio said, "The snails live there." Moving in closer, he spread the grass, uncovering several small ones, about the size of a dime, clinging to the sturdy blades of grass. But since it was already late morning and the sun was hot, the big ones, more sensitive to heat than the smaller ones, were descending from the grass to the ground.

"That's what they do during the day," Antonio said. "At night, when it is cool, they climb up again to feed. To get the big ones, which have the most meat, we should be here by six or seven o'clock in the morning."

As I began to look for snails to pick, Antonio gave me instructions. "Part the grass with one hand and pick with the other."

It occurred to me that Antonio and I were doing what man had been doing for several thousand years in the valley of Guadix—just as the American Indians had picked blueberries for many centuries before the Europeans arrived in the New World. Collecting snails, though, was much more comfortable work than blueberry picking. There were no brambles, poison ivy, or mosquitoes ready to harass the picker. Flies, to be sure, but not biting ones. Also, it went much faster. But snail-picking had its disadvantages. Our feet were soon wet from the irrigation water that seeped down the banks. Also, it was hot even though we were in the shade part of the time. We were soon sweating.

I continued to puzzle over Antonio's outburst in the bar. I gradually realized that it was because he was jealous. It wasn't just the use of *jillar* and *cal* that bothered him. It was my relationship with Manuel and Pepe. He saw himself as the person responsible for introducing me to Gypsy life and looked on others as intruders. Taking me snail hunting not only separated me from them, but re-tied the bond between us—as learning to eat with my fingers in his cave had helped to establish it.

In one and a half hours, by noon, we had picked about three pounds of snails including ten big ones.

"Let's sit down," said Antonio, selecting a shady spot under a large tree.

"You know," he continued, "we have enough to feed the family. Do you want to eat them with us?"

I said that I did, and later verified his estimate on the number of people the snails would feed.

Another side of Antonio's character surfaced when I asked him about snakes in the countryside.

"There are snakes," he said. "But they don't bother me, because I have a small *herradura* (horsehoe) on my belt."

He said this seriously, and when I looked at his belt, I saw that it was true. He was wearing a horseshoe (to be accurate, a burroshoe since it was small) over his belt buckle.

It was too late to pick any more snails. The sun was high and even the small ones were descending from the green leaves to the cool soil below. It was then that Antonio demonstrated his skill at foraging. Although his family hadn't been nomads for a long time, he still remembered the techniques of living off the land. He wasn't the only Gypsy in Guadix to employ the skills of a poacher. I once saw three *gitanas* picking peaches from privately owned land. But there were no families in Guadix like the Gypsy family who lived in the cave complex above the city of Baza. It was notorious for night-time thefts of produce and poultry from farms in the rich valley below.

"The chickens are our friends. They come to us freely," the head of the family said to me after having completed a successful raid the previous evening. His only shame was that one chicken had escaped.

"That one," he said, "didn't like us."

Walking past pear, apple and plum trees, Antonio first checked the ground for edible fruit. If there were none, he picked the fruit from a low-hanging branch. For fruit higher in the tree, he would give one of the big branches a few helpful shakes and then gather up the fallen fruit. He did this in a casual way, almost without stopping, to give the impression to any on-looker that we were simply strolling through the orchard, uninterested in the ripe fruit around us. When passing tomato plants, without losing stride, he quickly bent over and picked off ripe tomatoes, handing me the choicest ones. I ate them at once, as he did. I also picked a tomato or two and some loose fruit on the ground. Once, near a house, he cautioned me to put a pear he had given me into my pocket. Antonio pointed to a large shady tree. "It's a *mora*."

I looked and saw the branches were full of small berries, like blackberries. I tasted the fruit. It was delicious. Soon, though, I was so full that I had to beg off eating anything else. I was relieved that no stray chickens came near us for fear that they might have "asked to be caught."

As we returned to the city, our sacks laden with snails and our stomachs crammed with fruit, it came to me that what we had done had once caused farmers of Guadix to fear the Gypsies. We hadn't stolen any livestock, though, as the wandering Gypsies of another era might have done. It was these Gypsies the gentle poet Ramón Jiménez had in mind when he hurriedly put his donkey Platero into the safety of his yard on the arrival of Gypsies in Moguer, calling out to him, "Inside, Platero! Inside! I am going to close the street door for they are coming to take you away!"

We passed my hotel and entered the bar of Joaquín through a screen of dangling beads which kept out some of the flies. Some Castilian clients, seeing our sacks of snails, jokingly offered to buy them. We probably could have sold them for about $2.25, a profitable hour and a half's work for a laborer in Guadix.

I enjoyed this bar. Joaquín was a pleasant, rosy-faced person in his mid-thirties who always greeted me with a warm handclasp. He rarely showed the fatique he felt from standing behind his bar from early morning until midnight. Before we had time to order, he gave us two glasses of freshly made *sangría* to sample — on the house. Along with it came two *tapas* of spicy, hot meat on small pieces of bread. Later in the afternoon, he served hot, baked potatoes with his drinks.

We moved to the back of the bar with our *sangría* and *tapas*, and sat down on low chairs with our backs resting against casks of wine. Antonio used the toothpick, which held the meat of the *tapas* to the bread, to pick his teeth and to clean his finger nails. All I wanted was to relax in the coolness of the bar, enjoy another glass of *sangría*, and to carry on a desultory conversation with Antonio and with some of the old Castilian men sitting next to us. I had had enough "little adventures" for the morning: the Caló poem, the abrupt leave-taking from my Fonelas friends, the snail-picking and the foraging.

Antonio felt the same way, and we drowsily passed away an hour or so together, occasionally waving to acquaintances who came in and stood at the bar. We were unaware that the day's activity would lead to a threat against Antonio, which, in turn, would reveal to me a hidden characteristic of the Gypsy personality.

# 15

# "Mas Feo Que Un Gitano"
## (Uglier Than A Gypsy)

I call out to God,
'We are so few
We poor Calé.'

FLAMENCO VERSE

The night after the day we went snail-picking, I climbed in the darkness up the narrow trail leading to Antonio's cave where I was going to eat the snails we had picked. I passed one cave where the sound of flamenco from an old record was smothered by a skinny dog barking outside the cave entrance. I arrived at Antonio's about ten o'clock. Using the Caló word for night or evening I called out,

"*Hola! Buen arachí.*"

At the entrance to the cave, I pushed aside the cloth hanging over the doorway and descended the two steps into the foyer.

"Are you hungry?" asked Antonio. "Isabel is ready to cook the snails now. Ever since I brought them home they have been setting with a handful of flour spread over them to clean them out."

I gave him the bottle of wine I had brought.

Isabel, who had been awaiting my arrival, threw a handful of salt onto the snails followed by a cup of vinegar, mixing everything thoroughly with her hands for several minutes. Following six or seven cold-water rinses, she put them on the stove to boil for an hour. After the boiling, she washed them again, and then began the final step. This was to fry them for fifteen minutes with crushed peppers, almonds and a little garlic. The fragrant odor filled the kitchen.

(I later told María, the cook in the Hotel Comercio, about Isabel's preparation. The hotel never served snails, but María was interested because she cooked them for her family in her cave home. She said that her technique was the same as Isabel's except that she added toasted bread when she fried them.

Isabel put the hot frypan full of snails, juice and peppers onto the table. This was our dinner, along with a round loaf of bread. I looked at Antonio to see how to start. He broke off a hunk of bread and dunked it into the juice in the pan. I did the same, letting the bread soak up the liquid. It was delicious. Antonio then put some pins on the table for picking the meat from the shell. (He, himself, somehow extracted the meat with his teeth.) Joselito, who had been impatiently waiting to begin, grabbed a pin and attacked the snails. He loved them and showed it. Soon his empty shells were scattered over the floor where he threw them. They landed so rapidly that they sounded like shots from a machine gun. Isabel then sat down, and the four of us, drinking some wine, ate for half an hour or so until we could eat no more — there were still snails left in the pan when we stopped eating.

"You liked them," Isabel said.

"*Sí. Es un buen balichón.*" (Yes. It's a good meal.)

I had answered truthfully. I had enjoyed them even though this was the first time I had ever eaten snails in such a large quantity.

Sometime during the meal I had sensed the family was tense. When we were almost finished eating, Antonio confirmed my feeling. "We have a problem," he said.

Isabel nodded.

"It's the fault," Antonio continued, "of the *payo guarda del campo*. (non-Gypsy agricultural guard.) Yesterday when we were picking snails, a land-owner reported to the guard patroling the cultivated crops and irrigation ditches, that I stole fruit and vegetables, particularly corn."

I suppose that the accusation was legally correct, because Antonio and I had taken produce that didn't belong to us, although we had taken very little — and no corn. I preferred to look at it from the Gypsy point of view. We had taken only what we could eat. There was, of course, no protest about picking the snails. Landowners were pleased to have them thinned out because of the damage they did to crops.

"This afternoon," said Antonio, "the *guarda* spoke to me in the city below. He said he is going to notify the *jundunaré*."

"Did you ask him what proof he had?"

"Yes. He said the land-owner identified me by my yellow shirt. He also said that there was a tall *extranjero* with me."

"What happens now?"

"The *chungalo* can fine me one thousand pesetas (about twenty dollars), and send me to the *estiribel*."

*Chungalo*, another word for Guardia Civil, means ugly in Caló. *Estiribel* is the origin of the slang word "stir" for jail.

Once Antonio and Isabel had explained the charges, we had to decide on a course of action. When I volunteered my services, I was drawn further under the umbrella of the family. But what should my role be? A friend of the family? An uncle of the children? (I found later that it was considered by some Gypsies to be a more intimate role.) And what was there that a foreigner could do to help Antonio? I had no influence in the city. I had purposefully avoided the Guardia whose function was to enforce laws that Gypsies often disobey.

Remembering the warnings from my Castilian friends about dealing with Gypsies, and the early episode of the *Hokkano Baro*, I considered the possibility that this might be a lead-in for a more complex trick, such as a request to advance money for Antonio's fine. But I dismissed this thought. Our relationship was too far advanced for another *jojana bara*—and I was correct in this conclusion. Neither Antonio nor Isabel asked me for money then—or ever again for that matter.

Then I wondered if this were a trial to check my worthiness to remain close to the family. It was possible, but I felt it was beyond the ability of Antonio and Isabel to play a scene throughout the evening with such a high level of intensity. So I entered wholeheartedly into the discussion to find a solution.

Antoino wasted no time. *"Abiya conmigo a la jundunaré?"* (Will you come with me to the Guardia Civil?)

I thought for a moment while juggling brown-skinned Joselito on my lap. Then, since Antonio had used two Caló words *abiya* and *jundunaré*, I replied with another. *"Nahelo."*

I could not have anticipated it, then, but my agreement to visit the office of the Guardia set a precedent for my going there at a future date on a matter of even more urgency to the family.

I also offered to get advice from a new acquaintance, a retired officer from the Guardia Civil. But Antonio said, "Not yet." He wanted to devise a line of defense. "I don't have any hogs. They eat most of the corn in the region. I have only a goat and goats don't get fed corn."

During the conversation, I realized that I had made another discovery about the Gypsies of Guadix. Antonio and Isabel were deciding on a course of action without outside help, except for my small contribution. There was no "Big Man" or chief that Gypsies in other countries turn to for intercession with the authorities. The "Big Man," as Rena Gropper described him in her *Gypsies in the City*, is the head of several related families he assists when they are in trouble. Nor was there a "king of the Gypsies," a favorite figure of the press in other countries.

Isabel, who had been in and out of the cave while doing some washing outside, joined us in the kitchen where Antonio and I had been drinking wine. She was bending over the butane stove while cooking our dinner. Suddenly she straightened up and screamed,

*"Es má feo que un gitano!"* (He's uglier than a Gypsy!)

It was a dramatic moment. It became quiet in the cave. This was not the Isabel I knew—the gentle and demure housewife. Nor was it the Isabel who acted out the role of the arrogant *gitana* along the streets of Guadix, concealing her sensitivity to the hostility of her audience of shopkeepers. This was a fiery *gitana* whose scream of desperation filled the room.

Their enemy was "uglier than a Gypsy."

I was stunned. Though what she said may appear to be of little moment, she had bared a Gypsy soul to me—an outsider. I didn't know how to handle this development. I had read about Jews carrying racial scars, but nothing about Gypsies. They were supposed to be too thick-skinned. Only a few years ago, when planning my voyage among the Gypsies, I had questioned my ability to get acquainted with them. Yet here I was in the heart of a Gypsy family, not only privy to its reaction to a crisis that endangered its well-being, but I was taking part in solving it. This was more than I had bargained for. If in the quiet of my home I subconsciously had been looking for a carefree Gypsy world in Spain, I had found something different.

What I remembered telling myself at the start was to learn what I could about Gypsy life, what a normal observer would see, how the Gypsies dressed, what they did for a living. I had not anticipated this plunge below the surface. I hadn't expected to look into the soul of a Gypsy and find suffering. Would these depths be too much for me? More than I could bear? In my everyday contacts with Antonio and Isabella and with Carlos the smith and with Luis de los Caballos, would I be able to subdue the churning which I now felt?

I thought of an American friend who after an evening of listening to *cante jondo* or deep song from which flamenco developed, swore that he would never be exposed to it again. "It reaches too far into me," he said. "I fear it. It is too disturbing." But I could not leave this Gypsy family and my other Gypsy friends. I had learned to love them. Although I could never suffer as they did, I could share the pain that they endured. I needed them, probably more than they needed me, for they had taught me things about myself that I never realized were there.

The silence in the cave continued. One of us had to break it, so trying to appear casual, I asked Isabel to repeat what she had said, pretending not to have understood the first time. Embarrassed, she repeated it, but in a much softer tone. Antonio elaborated on her meaning. "She was referring to the guard. She means that his skin is darker than a Gypsy's." For emphasis, he touched my skin, saying how light it was, even though to me it was fairly dark, having been tanned by the Andalusian sun. Isabel nodded in agreement. This made no sense, though, for the guard was a fair-complexioned man, "un-Gypsy looking." Furthermore, skin color was not an issue as in America. For example, Falcó, when cataloguing the faults of the Gypsies, did not include their darkness as one of them.

Why had it taken me so long to discover this silent sorrow? Shouldn't I have sensed it, even before Isabel's cry had thrust it upon me? I had overlooked the clues. There were the flamenco stanzas about broken souls screaming their grief:

*Son tan grandes mis penas*
*que no caben más. Ay! Ay! Dios mío!*

My sorrows are so great
that I can bear no more. Oh! My God!

and from Lorca's *Ballad of the Black Pain*, "Oh pain, pain of the Gypsies...pain from a hidden spring..."

I also remembered an afternoon in the plaza of a small village when I was hailed by a drunken Gypsy about sixty years old who was sitting on a bench with a nondescript dog at his feet. He followed me into a nearby bar where the owner, a little man over whom the Gypsy towered, calmly refused to serve him. "You have had enough, Santiago."

"But I want to buy *el señor* a drink."

"*Mañana*," I replied to the owner's relief.

Santiago, on hearing my reply, began a garbled monologue, "We are all poor. We have nothing." And using *feo* as Isabel had, he added, "We are *feo, feo.*"

Several years later I was to have further confirmation of this Gypsy self-mockery caused by the low esteem in which they are held in Spain. It was in Morón de la Frontera where I was visiting the family of the Gypsy guitarist Diego del Gastor, famous in the world of flamenco. His bed-ridden brother-in-law, pointing to a weak sun trying to pierce a cloudy sky, said to me, "Do you know what that sun is called? *Es el sol de los gitanos, porque no vale nada como los gitanos.*" (It's a Gypsy sun, because it's worthless like the Gypsies.) Yet, he was proud of being a Gypsy.

In the cave, Isabel's anger had returned, and putting her face close to me she said in a strained voice, "The *jundunaré* to whom the *guarda* will report Antonio are the ones who get all the good fruit."

"And the good jobs when they retire," added Antonio.

"Why don't they and the others leave us alone?" Isabel asked. "We are good people. Look at Antonio and me. We love each other, and have nice children. We bother no one."

She then grabbed the long-handled mop with which she scrubbed the floors, and holding it above her head shook it vigorously, shouting, "They are *chuqueles* (dogs)!"

Tears came to her eyes and she began to sob. Although emotionally drained, she had a final epithet for the Guardia. "They are *chute!*" she called out in a husky voice. *Chute* is Caló for milk, but here Isabel was giving it another of its meanings, "semen."

Antonio, who rarely showed affection toward Isabel, moved to her side and put his arms around her. Joselito did the same. I could find nothing to say. Isabel had exposed to me, a stranger, the depth of the Gypsy soul, and I did not want to risk destroying her trust with a commonplace remark.

The rest of the evening was an anti-climax. Isabel regained her composure, and set some food on the table. As we ate in silence, I realized that I should not have been surprised that it was Isabel rather than Antonio, who had revealed the family's torment. It was Isabel and the other *gitanas* who, having taken it onto themselves to exhibit their Gypsiness to the middle class, were exposed to their dislike, and so carried deeper wounds than *gitanos*. It wasn't that Antonio and the other male Gypsies did not share this inner sorrow; it was that the women felt it more.

After eating, Antonio and I made plans for handling the emergency.

When I parted, we left it (I use the "we" intentionally since I had become one of the actors in the family crisis) that we would not act until the *Guarda* made his move. The possibility existed that he had only been threatening Antonio to prevent his taking fruit again. If so, he might not press charges with the Guardia Civil. Time proved we were correct. The days went by without further threats from the *Guarda*, and after a few weeks had passed, it was apparent that Antonio was not to be prosecuted.

As I dwelt on the incident in the cave that night, I realized that Antonio and Isabel had not been concerned about the Guardia Civil's getting the best fruit or the agricultural guard's being darker or uglier than a Gypsy. It went deeper. Isabel's wail of despair was not that of a lone *gitana*. It was a cry from the heart of the Gypsy race; it came from a people's realization that they must ever be apart because of their pride of race; it was a cry of frustration at the injustices and suffering experienced as slaves in Hungary and death under Hitler; it was the voice of a people who for a thousand years have refused to conform, and who are, as the poet in Falcó's shop expressed it, "A race that suffers the consequences of its liberty."

# 16

# To Granada's Sacromonte

I was driving Antonio to Granada to see his grandmother who was ill in a hospital. Though Granada was only a little over thirty miles from Guadix, it was more than an hour's drive on the narrow, twisting road which ran through the Sierra Harana, a chain of mountains paralleling Spain's highest range, the Sierra Nevada. I loved this drive. It was one of the most scenic routes in all of Spain, and I never tired of looking at the snow-covered Sierra off to the left and at the bold, rocky peaks to the right. It wasn't a highway to rush along, but for a person not in a hurry, it was a delight.

We had been driving for about twenty-five minutes, and not long after passing the hill village of Diezma, we approached a settlement of several houses known as the Venta del Molinillo, the Inn of the Little Mill. Just above the venta in a cluster of shacks Manuel del Molinillo, a folk healer, practices. Antonio pointed to several patients standing around an open fire waiting for him.

He then surprised me by saying, "We are together, just the two of us."

He was letting me know that he liked being with me, and also pointing out that it was unusual for us not to be in a group. In Guadix, Gypsies and non-Gypsies love company, and two people chatting in the street or in a bar are soon joined by others.

"Yes," I replied. "*Como quiribós.*" (Like friends.)

We were quiet again. I didn't bother to tell Antonio that several hundred years ago his ancestors had known this high mountainous country well, wandering along its peaks and passes, and sometimes even controlling its traffic. A reminder of those far-away days is the name of a 6000-foot range of mountains above the pass, the Cuerda de los Gitanos.

We soon saw the famous plain which extends outward from Granada. Around the next bend the ochre towers of the Alhambra palace appeared beyond the Albaycin hill.

"*Qué vista!*" I said.

"*Sí,*" replied Antonio, "*Pero...*" and he reminded me that in Guadix he also had a splendid view, an ochre-walled Moorish castle to gaze at on the upper edge of the city of houses, and the city of Guadix with its huge cathedral to look down on.

When Antonio completed his hospital visit, it was only early afternoon.

"How would you like to go up to the Alhambra?" I asked. "I want to take some photographs across the Daro river of the Gypsy flamenco caves at Sacromonte from there."

"*Está bien.* I like having a *payo* driver."

I told Antonio the story about Gypsies casting cannon balls for the siege of Granada for the army of Ferdinand and Isabella. He wasn't impressed but when I told him that Emperor Carlos V was upset because Gypsies stole animals and clothing from houses in the city, his eyes lit up. "I taught you how to pick other peoples' fruit, you know," he said, referring to our foraging expedition when we had picked snails.

Back in the city we saw Gypsy bootblacks walking along the sidewalks.

"Your fellow workers," I said. "Why don't you come to Granada and make lots of money?"

"I don't like this city. Too much traffic. My friends are in Guadix."

Antonio, a son of Guadix as much as any non-Gypsy *guadijeño*, was confirming his love for the city of his birth. While I never developed his affection for the city, I had come to love its residents, and I was no longer disturbed by its unattractive appearance.

"Let's go up to Sacromonte for awhile," I said. At the Camino del Sacromonte a directional sign announced in large letters that this was the road to Sacromonte. Indicating that priorities have changed, the name of the abbey, once the goal of pilgrims, appeared in small letters. Pilgrims on foot have been replaced by limousines carrying tourists to Gypsy flamenco shows.

Standing at the corner were three Gypsy touts hustling business for flamenco performances. Offering to park our car, they called out the names of the establishments they represented: "Cueva 33! La Golondrina! La Fragua!" They looked as though they could not be trusted.

Antonio shared my feeling. "Do not stop!" he said. "It is not safe. It will cost too much."

I looked at him but made no comment.

"I don't like these people," he continued, and then for emphasis added, *"Por la gloria de mi madre!"* (For the love of my mother!)

He then assumed a stone-faced expression, looking straight ahead. He was in a Gypsy world, but one foreign to his experience. It made him feel ill at ease.

I drove slowly along the curving road passing the flamenco caves. Above one of them, the Cueva de la Rocío, a fantastic creation of white-washed concrete, worthy of appearing in a journal of art, shot upward. Rolling layers of concrete were plastered for one hundred feet up the face of the hill to prevent erosion. The uneven placement of the various layers gave it the appearance of a gigantic sculpture.

In front of the Bar el Rojo, Antonio nudged me. "Look," he said, and pointed toward a sullen-looking Gypsy in his sixties who was eating an orange and throwing the peelings onto the street. By his side sat a caricature of a *gitana*, her fat body covered with a bright green blouse and a long, blue skirt. Her face was heavily made up, and an ugly comb was set high in her hair. I had never seen a Gypsy like her in Guadix.

Just before the Bar La Bulería we passed a tiny, windowless shed with smoke pouring out through its door.

"It must be an *herrero* (smith)," I said to Antonio. "Let's stop!"

We walked up to the doorway and looked inside. My hunch was correct. A smith was at work, a tall, thin Gypsy about sixty years old. With his left hand he operated a bellows; with his right he was striking out rings from hot iron on a make-shift forge. The four legs of the fire box rested perilously on a pile of loosely placed bricks, and the anvil was balanced on a stump of wood.

The smith, whose name was José, told us that he was the last *herrero* on Sacromonte.

As we left this lone survivor of the many Gypsy smiths who had once worked in the hills above Granada, I addressed the ghost of García Lorca (he died in 1936) who had last seen Granada's Gypsies in the mid-1930s. "Yes, Federico—and all the other poets, artists and composers who have been moved to express the motion and sound of Gypsy smiths working at their forges—smoke and sparks still fly from a Gypsy anvil on Sacromonte, but I fear not for many years longer."

Beyond the flamenco caves, we entered a cave bar and ordered wine from a Castilian woman. Bunches of medicinal herbs for sale hung on the wall, camomile for the stomach and spike lavender for the liver. When the husband came in, he showed us around the cave. It had twelve rooms! On the wall above the bar a sign read:

*Si bebes para olvidar*
*paga antes de empezar.*
If you drink to forget
pay before you start.

As we were returning to the flamenco area, a Gypsy in his early twenties shouted, "Antonio! Antonio!" A cousin of Antonio, he invited us to a performance in a cave at a "special" price for me and free to Antonio. Antonio, still suspicious of Sacromonte Gypsies, was not enthusiastic, but I accepted.

The cave was full of German tourists. While waiting for the show to begin, I thought about the origin of flamenco and its predecessor *cante jondo*. To Lorca, it was the voice of antiquity, the voice of the Jew, the Arab, and the Gypsy. Its roots were not in Granada, but in Cádiz and Jerez de la Frontera. Granada's contribution, a university professor had told me, was in preserving it.

Guadix, in a small way, also helped to preserve flamenco. Two fandangos originated in the region —one in the village of La Peza and one in Dólar. I have been to these villages, and when I learned the music was originally Arabic, I wasn't surprised. The villages looked Moorish.

The guitarist began to play and three youthful *gitanas* snapped their fingers, clapped their hands and tapped their feet. One plump, middle-aged woman, her mouth brightened with lipstick, sang while another struck the tambourine. A young dancer sprang from her chair to dance in the center of the cave. She was wearing a long-sleeved, maroon dress, that hugged her slender waist and hips before falling in two ruffles to below the knees. The natural brown of her skin was accentuated by rouged cheekbones; her eyebrows were penciled and her eyes shaded. She danced well, although she lacked the intensity of the bare-footed Lola in the caves of Guadix.

I looked at Antonio. He was wearing his detached expression. As a Gypsy from Guadix, he was not permitting himself to be carried away. Catching my look, he shrugged his shoulders. He did, though, politely clap his hands.

When the dancer had finished, and while the spectators were applauding, Antonio and I thanked his cousin and left the cave. We had a long drive through the mountains ahead of us. It was dark outside, but across the Darro we could see the walls and towers of the Alhambra lit by the moon.

Leaving the camino, we drove up through the Albaycin onto the highway to Guadix. On the long climb to the mountains ahead, we exchanged a few remarks but for the most part were silent. Handling the car required my attention. Despite occasional help from the moon, the road at night was difficult to drive on. There were few guardrails to prevent the unwary driver from sliding into steep ravines.

I thought about Antonio's earlier remark that day. "We are alone. The two of us." I wondered if George Borrow's Gypsy guide of one hundred and forty years ago—also an Antonio—would have made a similar comment. Borrow's Antonio was from Badajoz where I also met an Antonio, a money changer. Borrow's trip with him was from Badajoz to Madrid, much farther than from Guadix to Granada. But I had spent more time with my Antonio—not on long trips, but on many short ones. Borrow's Antonio comes to us as a shadow person, a kind of dream figure. My Antonio was more down-to-earth. He, too, was a guide, but not on the road to Granada. He was a guide to Gypsy life and customs.

I had questioned his Gypsiness. With his olive skin, slight stature and balding head, he didn't seem to be much of a Gypsy. He lacked the bronzeness of Camilo and the other Gyspies of Fonelas. He wasn't as sharp as Luis de los Caballos, or as articulate as el Golondrina, or as dignified as Carlos the smith. I thought, would another Gypsy have been a better pilot to the intricate lore of the Gypsy world? There were Gypsies who knew more Caló and who were more Gypsy looking, but Antonio's loyalty could not have been easily duplicated. To be sure, Antonio had encouraged a *jojana bara* on me when Rosario and Rodrigo posed as his parents, but that was because he was as much at a loss on how to deal with me as I was with him. He had followed his tradition, which called for taking advantage of the unwary stranger.

As for his Gypsiness, Antonio recognized that he wasn't Gypsy looking, and it bothered him. "My face isn't as dark as some Gypsies," he told me. Yet he looked on himself as being more Gypsy than Manuel, one of the bronze Gypsies from Fonelas, as I found when he became incensed over the off-color poem Manuel and Pepe del Bigote had written for me. "I am more Gypsy than they are!" he had said. A

*The author with Antonio, his loyal guide to the Gypsy world, and son, Joselito, amongst the elegant chimneys of the cave city.*

poem by a Barcelona Gypsy described his attitude perfectly:

> I have pride in being a Gypsy
> It is not based on tambourine and flamenco
> But like religious relics
> Rests on the heart.

Antonio also had been doing some thinking about our relationship, and when I stopped the car to get a drink of water at the spring in the Puerto de la Mora, he said, "*Soy muy formal con tigo.*" He was telling me that he was honest with me.

"I know it," I replied. "I can trust you."

Since the early days of our acquaintance when the *jojana bara* occurred, he had not tried to use me for a selfish purpose. On the contrary, he had declined some of my offers to aid him, even rejecting the use of the trunk of my automobile to carry grass for his goat, because it would soil the car.

"And haven't I shown you how Gypsies live?" he asked.

"Yes, you have, Antonio. You took me into your cave and introduced me to Isabel and Joselito."

"And to Ramón de la Toñica," he added.

"Where I met your friends, *payos*, as well as *gitanos*, and for all of this I am indebted to you. You are my friend."

We had expressed our feelings honestly but not emotionally. I am reserved, and so was Antonio. Neither of us had the gregarious nature of el Golondrina or little Antonio the guide. For the most part, we had to rely on our actions to show our affection for each other. I revealed affection in my love for his children and by supporting the family when it needed help. Antonio revealed his in his openness about Gypsy life. Later, while driving along the level stretch of the pass, I said, "Well, what did you think of the evening?"

Antonio hesitated for a few moments. He leaned toward me so that his face was closer to mine. When he replied, this ordinary bootblack, who did not look as Gypsy as the dark, long-haired picaroons of the Camino del Sacromonte, began with, "*Nosotro tenemo má cojone que lo de Grana* (We Gypsies in Guadix have more courage than the ones in Granada)."

After a pause he added, "I don't like the way they act. We are different. We are more Gypsy."

And the more sophisticated Gypsies of Sacromonte would probably have agreed with his claim of superiority, for they, like the Calé elsewhere, look on the Guadix Gypsies as the most Gypsy-like in the entire province of Granada.

# 17

# A Gypsy Drama

I had thought often about the bloody scene in front of the gun store on the main street of Guadix, which the old *marchante* had described to me. (Chapter Three) The death of the Benalúa Gypsy from the knives of the Alcudia horse traders had happened because of family honor. And while honor is frequently at the heart of Gypsy feuds, Lorca in "The Death of Antoñito el Camborio" along the river Guadalquivir has another motif, envy, lead to Antoñito's death. When Antoñito is asked who snatched his life away, he replies that it was his four cousins Heredia—what they did not envy in others they envied in him.

The reader, though, does not learn what caused the envy of the cousins, because Antonio soon dies—in his three bursts of blood. Was he popular with women? This would have aroused envy. And was he also perhaps disloyal or cruel to his wife who may have been an Heredia? The combination of envy and anger over mistreatment of his wife, a violation of family honor, could have led the Heredia cousins to attack him, because, as I had learned, disruption of family relationships has long been a cause of bloody quarrels among Gypsies.

I would be one of the central characters in a similar Gypsy family dispute, in which envy and honor were intertwined. The principal players would be:

| | |
|---|---|
| Antonio, the bootblack | The Gorilla, a cousin of Antonio |
| Isabel, his wife | Antonio's mother |
| Luis, Antonio's 18 year old brother | Falcó |
| | Myself |

The opening scene took place on an early spring morning in March. Men were wearing leather jackets for protection against the cool wind blowing from the Sierra. I had gone into the indoor market, crowded with shoppers, to say hello to Pepe el Pando at his fruit-vegetable stand. He had just returned from having his mid-morning brandy. "Your friend Antonio is next door in the Bar el Canario," he said. I thanked him and went to the bar. Antonio and Luis were standing at the far end. They looked as disreputable as only Gypsies can when they are so inclined. Both had a stubble of beard on their faces. Antonio's trousers were dirty and Luis' red sweater was full of holes.

As soon as the bartender had set a glass of wine and a *tapa* of hot meat in front of me, Antonio said, "A bad thing has happened."

My first thought was that one of his children or Isabel had become ill.

"One of my cousins said that you have had sexual relations with Isabel, and that you are the father of our Antonio (his fair-skinned two year old)."

"This is incredible!" I said.

"Yes," replied Antonio, "and it can lead to a *chinga* with *churís* (a knife fight)."

Before I could react, the usual happened. Two people joined us.

I needed time to think and to be alone so I excused myself and went to the park where I strolled under the trees and around the statue of Guadix' most famous son, Pedro de Alarcón, whose novel *The Three Cornered Hat* became de Falla's composition of the same name and Diaghilev's ballet. Alarcón would never have found himself in the predicament that I was. Well-bred gentlemen of his era did not associate with Gypsies anymore than did the store owners of today.

As I thought about the accusation of Antonio's cousin, its full implication sank in. It struck at the integrity of the family, the heart of Gypsy life, which centers on the *gitana's* loyalty and faithfulness toward her husband. That is why an extra-marital affair by a *gitana*, especially with a *payo*, is viewed by other Gypsies as one of the worst crimes she can commit.

I was forced to do some soul-searching. I reviewed my relationship with Antonio and Isabel to see if I could identify a particular episode that might have triggered the accusation. Had I greeted Isabel too openly in the city of houses? Had my strolling through the fair-grounds with the family the previous September caused tongues to wag? It had seemed innocent enough. Joselito was holding one hand and Antonia, the daughter of Black Beret, the other. *Payos*, though, do not walk in public with Gypsy families, and the next day Falcó said, "I hear you went to the fair with the Gypsies."

"Yes," I replied, "but the little girl was a *paya*."

Since Gypsies, for their part, do not stroll with non-Gypsies in the city, some of them may have resented this display of affection between Gypsy and *payo*. Perhaps it was acceptable to have quiet contacts with a Gypsy family in the cave area, but not to broadcast it in the city below where it might give other *payos* ideas of developing closer relations with the Gypsies. I had, it seems, violated taboos of both groups.

These thoughts were running through my mind when I walked to Falcó's shop and confided in him what Antonio had told me. He reacted spontaneously, bursting out with:

Ah, you see! You cannot trust these people.
Beware! A knife will come next,
And then a demand for money.
Stay away from them. Beware!

Urging me not to tell anyone else, he quietly discussed the situation with a friend in the court system who then gave me the same admonition—and in almost the identical language, as though from a chorus in a Greek tragedy.

Take care...your life is in danger...
They are not to be trusted.

My inital reaction was to scoff at these warnings. Wasn't I friend of the Gypsies? particularly of Antonio? Hadn't they referred to me as "one of the family?" But then I began to have second thoughts. I knew about Gypsies knife-fighting over a point of honor. Wasn't the safest course of action to follow the advice of Falcó and stop seeing the family? This would prevent me from becoming another Antoino Torres Heredia, dying with three bursts of blood.

It was also possible, though, that there was only slight danger of bloodshed, and that, as Falcó had suggested, it was a blackmail operation, a real *Hokkano Baro*, a swindle of a grand order. Soon Antonio or Luis would be asking me for money to buy off the rumor mongers. But I had known Antonio too long to believe that. He would no longer attempt a hoax as he had done in the early days of our acquaintance.

I found that Falcó had another concern. It was the fear of my being ridiculed.

"This affair is terrible!" he said. "People will believe the accusation. They will say, 'There goes the *extranjero* who is the father of a Gypsy child.' "

To him, as a member of the middle class, it would be shameful to be accused of siring a child by a *gitana*. Ridicule of me could be transferred to him, since he was my friend. I understood his position, although I did not share it. Though I respected his views, our experiences in life had been different. I had not faced the years of real or fancied aggravations from Gypsies that he had. There was little I could say. And he would not have understood that had my life gone differently, I could have married a Gypsy and had Gypsy children.

Falcó's concern was based on a long established Spanish trait. Fernando Díaz-Playa in *The Spaniard and the Seven Deadly Sins* writes that the fear of ridicule, firmly rooted in the Spanish personality, governs most of the Spaniard's reactions. He quotes a Spanish proverb, "Better to be a cuckold without anyone knowing than not be one when everyone thinks you are." For the present situation, a little substituting in the proverb would have satisfied Falcó, "Better to be the father of a Gypsy child without anyone knowing than not to be one when everyone thinks you are."

Despite Falcó's concern, I decided to continue seeing Antonio and Isabel. I appreciated his advice, but I felt that I was too far committed to withdraw from the relationship. They were depending on my support.

Having made up my mind, I was uncertain what course to follow in these unmapped waters. While I was *"de la familia,"* I was not an *aratí* (blood) Gypsy. Had I been, I would have sought out the cousin and challenged him. Since I was not, the obligation for action was Antonio's, not mine.

The day after Antonio had told me about the *"mala cosa,"* I met him standing in front of the Bar Molinillo with his shoe-shine kit. "Tell me more about your cousin who made the accusation."

"He's a gorilla," Antonio said.

"What do you mean?"

"He looks like a gorilla. He's squat, and has a broad chest and shoulders."

"What does he do?"

"He unloads goods at the market."

Antonio's mother joined us and we strolled toward the park. She was sympathizing with Antonio when blind Rodrigo and his wife Rosario, walking arm-in-arm, joined us, their hands full of lottery tickets. I shook hands with Rodrigo, and bought a few tickets.

"Such bad language that man used," Rodrigo said.

Rosario nodded her head in agreement. She said, "We just visited Isabel en route to the city. She's sobbing over the terrible lie."

Later, other Gypsies expressed their sympathy. "It is nonsense!" said el Golondrina. Wild Concha, Isabel's sister, was prepared to go beyond simply showing sympathy, and had to be quieted down by Isabel. But the most telling support was so subtle that I was not fully aware of it until afterwards. Carlos the smith arranged it. Knowing that I wanted to take his picture, the next day when I stopped to chat with him on the sidewalk across from the Bar Molinillo, where he displayed his wrought-iron articles, he told me that he would be at the cave of his nephew Rafael late that afternoon.

When I arrived, a small fiesta was going on in front of the cave. Carlos and his wife were there along with Rafael and several other Gypsies. One of the men—only men were dancing—was performing with abandon. He was short and wide-shouldered like Pepe el Pando. I didn't realize it then but this was the "Gorilla." Carlos had heard what he had said about Isabel and me, and had purposefully asked me to be present when the Gorilla was there. This let him know that Carlos did not believe in the rumor. It also meant that as guests of a mutual friend, the Gorilla and I shared in the drink, food and music of the fiesta, thus making it more difficult for him to continue to make remarks about me.

A few minutes after Rodrigo and Rosario had left to continue their rounds selling lottery tickets, Isabel rapidly walked up to us. Her features were composed. Her eyes had a steely look about them as though she had made up her mind what she was going to do, and would stand for no opposition. If she had been crying, she had removed the traces of tears.

With Gypsy directness, she said to Antonio, "I am going to the Guardia Civil."

"What is there to gain?" he asked.

"*Mucho!*" Isabel replied, vigorously nodding her head for emphasis, so that her pony tail waggled in back of her neck. Then, without any further discussion, she looked at me and said in a firm voice, "*Vámanos al coqué!*" (Let us go to the barracks of the Guardia!)

Because of the seriousness of the occasion, she assumed I would be willing to commit myself. She remembered the earlier incident with the agricultural guard when I had offered to speak to the Guardia Civil on Antonio's behalf.

Having announced her intention, she strode off toward the building of the Guardia detachment, which was in the direction of Almería about one hundred and fifty yards away. I had to make up my mind quickly whether or not to follow her. There was no time to reach a well thought-out decision, weighing the various considerations. I looked at Antonio for guidance, but he was of no help. He was reluctant to commit himself, and was gazing off into space with a feigned air of disinterest.

I turned and followed Isabel. It seemed to be the only decent thing to do, even though it placed me further into Gypsy life, with its accompanying obligations and danger. Not to have gone with her would have been cowardly—although safer. I hurried to catch up, and did so within a few steps. But where should I position myself in relation to her? *Payo* men don't walk alongside Gypsy women, but I didn't want to trail behind. I compromised by walking abreast, but with a safe interval between us, and keeping my eyes straight to the front as Isabel was doing and not speaking.

I also tried to appear unconcerned—if that were possible with a fiery *gitana* at my side—and oblivious to questioning looks from passers-by who sensed that something unusual was taking place. One of them, though, Pedro el Moro, walking by with one of his little girls, pretended we were not there. But the old Gypsy crone, la Estrella (the star), to whom I sometimes gave a few pesetas, stared directly at us from where she was sitting on the sidewalk. Her tongue would soon relate what she had seen. Still of no assistance was Antonio, who was lagging behind at a safe distance.

As we walked past the shop that sold hunting weapons, Armas y Municiones de Caza, I was reminded that this was the site of the terrible battle where Dulce's brother from Benalúa was killed by her husband. Was a similar episode about to take place?

In the few minutes it took to reach the Guardia detachment, my mind was racing rapidly. Perhaps Isabel was a throw-back to the period of a thousand years ago when the Gypsies, on leaving India, may have been a matriarchal society with the tribal chief and the tribal mother, the *phuri dai*, sharing in ruling the tribe. Or perhaps she had been lifted from a Greek tragedy. Whatever, she emerged as a courageous woman, prepared to take unusual action in defense of her honor and family.

Lorca, who describes the ruthlessness of the Guardia toward the Gypsies, would have understood the courage it took for her to go to their headquarters. The Guardia has long been the enemy of the Calé, because of their overzealous enforcement of the laws which Gypsies frequently break. Isabel knew nothing of Lorca and his imaginary city of the Gypsies, but she knew that the Gypsies avoided the Guardia, especially their quarters which we were rapidly approaching.

Arriving at the barracks, Isabel wheeled into the courtyard, with me a few feet behind. She strode into the waiting office where a sergeant was processing papers while several people were sitting and standing about the room. She addressed him in a loud voice, "I wish to see the Commandante!"

The sergeant, surprised at such a strange request from a *gitana*, was about to tell her that the Commandante was busy, and that she would have to wait her turn. But Isabel gave him no opportunity to put her off. With her eyes boring into his with Gypsy fierceness, she said, "A cousin of my husband is telling people that this *extranjero* is the father of my children."

Her intensity made the sergeant realize that this was no ordinary dispute which could be put off for an hour or two. So instead of asking her to sit down and wait with the others, he got up from his chair, walked to the door of the Commandante's office, knocked and entered. He returned almost immediately. "You may enter," he said.

The Commandante stood up from behind his desk above which hung a large photograph of Franco. Courteously receiving us, he inquired what the problem was. As soon as he understood the nature of the incident, he said that he would like to talk to Isabel alone, so I left and returned to the sergeant's office. The sergeant moved close to me, and said in a low voice, "You have nothing to worry about."

I thanked him. It was kind of him to reassure me, but he had misread the situation. He was referring to Spanish law, because his work life was governed by it. But my concern was not Spanish law; it was Gypsy law. And I was under no illusions that I was out of danger, according to the way the Gypsies viewed the situation.

From the waiting room, I could hear Isabel talking with the Commandante. I was surprised at his decency. He was not at all overbearing as I had expected. When Isabel came out of his office, she had calmed down. I said nothing to her as we left together, but Antonio, waiting on the sidewalk, asked, "How did it go?"

She seemed to feel reassured, but her only response was a nod of her head. She preferred to talk to him in the privacy of their cave. We continued along the sidewalk together until reaching the market when I turned up the street to my hotel. Before parting, Isabel said, "The Commandante wants to see Antonio in the morning."

The next day Antonio reported to me on his meeting with the Commandante. "He says there is not enough evidence. He says he can't take any action. Isabel and I are disappointed. We hoped the Guardia would lock up the Gorilla for saying these things."

I sympathized with Antonio, but I thought the Commandante had done all he could within the framework of the law. To me, Isabel's visit was more meaningful than any decision the Commandante might have reached. By going directly to the Guardia in an un-Gypsy like act, she had demonstrated to the other Gypsies how seriously she regarded the charge.

A few days after the Commandante declared that he could do nothing more about the incident, the action mounted to a level of violence. Antonio said to me when shining my shoes, "Last night the Gorilla had a fierce quarrel with my mother when he was passing her cave near the Ermita Nueva en route to his cave. He stopped, spoke savagely, and then struck her."

This was difficult for me to believe. I could not visualize a Gypsy of thirty striking a mother in her forties. (Antonio's mother was married when she was fourteen, could not have been much older when Antonio was born.) It seemed more likely that Antonio's mother had started the dispute, probably harassing the Gorilla as he walked in front of her cave. Whether or not he hit her, I would never know. It did seem, though, that a confrontation had taken place, and that a more serious one could be expected in the near future.

Was Falcó right? Were Isabel, Antonio and I in peril of assault from the Gorilla and other members of his family? Certainly I could feel tensions increasing. It did appear, though, that both Isabel and I were being eased out of the main stream of action, while Antonio's side of the family—up to now, limited to his mother—assumed more responsibility. It seemed to be a preparation for a more serious stage of the conflict with the sidelining of unessential characters: Isabel, because hand-to-hand fighting where death may result is usually limited to men; and myself, as a foreigner unfamiliar with Gypsy demands when honor is challenged.

But what about Antonio? Wasn't he still in the main stream? According to Gypsy tradition, shouldn't he be acting more aggressively, instead of relying on his wife and mother to avenge the insult? Antonio, though, was in a perplexing position. I was his friend. He knew there were no grounds for the Gorilla's accusation. If there had been, his course of action would have been obvious—just as it was for the Gypsy who exclaimed in a flamenco stanza:

> I would draw my knife
> To cut the face
> Of anyone who loved my wife.

And neither could Antonio criticize Isabel because of my entering his household. He had been the one to invite me into the family cave.

Finding myself alone for a few moments with Pedro el Moro in the Bar Calatrava, and learning that he had heard about the situation, I asked him what Antonio should do.

"He could challenge the Gorilla," he said, "but he probably won't. The Gorilla is too strong for Antonio, so in a fight of sheer strength Antonio would lose. And Antonio lacks the skill needed for a knife fight. I don't know what he will do."

I could have added that Antonio was not an Antoñito el Camborio, ready to leap into a fight of flashing knives.

Pedro, who knew Antonio's family well, continued, "Antonio is something like his father, who was a weak person and an alcoholic. Antonio and his brothers and sisters have little respect for him. The mother raised the family."

"What about Isabel?" I asked.

"Ah! She is different. She is strong-willed as is her mother."

This confirmed my own view of Isabel. I remembered how she carried herself in the city of houses and how she had exploded in fury at the field guard who had threatened to report Antonio to the Guardia Civil for pilfering fruit. She loved Antonio and willingly bore his children, but in moments of family crisis she was the stronger of the two.

"You stay away from the Gorilla," she told Antonio. "I don't want any flashing of knives between you and him or between us and his family."

Antonio had nodded his head in agreement, and concerned for my safety, said, "Don't talk to anyone about this outside the family."

And, except with Falcó and Pedro, I didn't.

Two days later when I walked past the indoor market, I saw Luis sitting on the curbing across the street. When I got closer, I noticed a long, fresh cut on the right side of his face.

"*Qué pasó?*" I asked.

"*Anoche. El Gorila...*" (Last night. The Gorilla.) he replied.

"Let's go into the Bar Calatrava," I said. "I want to hear more."

"Last night," said Luis, who lived in his mother's cave with his wife and two-year old daughter, "I was tired and went to bed early. I fell into a deep sleep when my daughter called to me, '*Pato! Pato!* That man is here!' "

Luis paused, thrusting his face close to mine, so that our eyes were only a few inches apart. "I jumped up, and ran to the entrance of the cave where the Gorilla and my mother were shouting at each other. I told the Gorilla to be quiet and to move along. He refused, so I took hold of his arms. He became angry, and jerked my hands away."

This triggered the fight, and they began to strike each other, falling to the ground, rolling over and over. Luis came out on top, but his opponent pulled a knife, slashing at Luis' face. Before he could inflict serious damage, though, neighbors, aroused by his mother's screams, separated them, and sent the Gorilla flying.

This was the climax of the drama. There was to be no more violence. Luis had successfully defended the family honor, although he had been wounded. The Gorilla had to serve time in jail for inciting the conflict.

In the weeks and months that followed the final act, I continued to think about the events of the drama and my role in them. I wondered why voices of death had not been heard along the river Guadix as they had along the Guadalquivir when Antoñito el Camborio died. The ingredients for inflaming two Gypsy families into violence were present: an unfounded accusation and the tarnishing of a woman's honor.

"The answer is," said Pedro, "that the Gorilla's charges were softened by the other Gypsies' support of Antonio, of Isabel and of you. His brothers wanted no part of it, so there was no all-out family feud. And, you see, since Antonio was never the aggressor, the Gorilla could exit without confronting Antonio. He saved face by giving Luis a shallow knife cut."

I was still puzzled, though, over why the Gorilla had made his charges about Isabel and me. He could have held nothing against me, because we had never met until the fiesta at Rafael's cave. But then one day the dying words of Antoñito el Camborio came to me, "What they did not envy in others, they envied in me." The Gorilla, envious of my relationship with Antonio and Isabel, decided to end it by spreading a malicious rumor. Unfortunately, he was partially successful. My relations with the family were interrupted. Although I continued to see Antonio regularly, it was in city bars or in Ramón de la Toñica's. He and Isabel were reluctant for me to go to their home for fear of causing further rumors, and it was several months before I again visited the family cave.

# Epilogue

Over ten years have passed since I began my journey through the Gypsy world, guided by Antonio the bootblack. The knowledge I acquired of the inner-workings of this world would appear to be an adequate reason for bringing the voyage to a finish. But I have been unable to do so. I cannot close the door onto Gypsy life, and when I am within my study 3500 miles from Spain, I find myself carrying on imaginary conversations: "*Cómo están los chaborós, Antonio?*" "*Qué tal, Pedro?*" "*Rafael, tapiamos mol?*" "*Qué ay, Manuel?*"

While I have achieved my goal, to meet the Gypsies and to be accepted by them, it has not been an end into itself. They let me enter their homes and their club, the tavern of Ramón de la Toñica. They, in turn, have entered my heart. They helped me make discoveries about myself: that I could get along with them; that I could accept them as they are; that I could appreciate the qualities which have enabled them to survive as a socially outcast people during their centuries in Spain.

My voyage is no longer a quest for the wild and unknown. It is a journey among friends whom I visit as often as I can. Its focus remains Andalusia, the Gypsy heartland, with its principal anchorage the old Roman-Arabic city of Guadix where I relax with Carlos the ex-smith, Pepe el Pando now retired, and Pedro el Moro unemployed. In the city of houses Miguel the waiter has lost his job to the owner's son, el Golondrina is still at the Bar Dólor, but Falcó has sold his store because of illness. In Benalúa I see Luis de los Caballos and dark Mauro, but the mailman who introduced me to them is in Alicante. Bronze Rafael and Gilberto the gravedigger are still in Fonelas and on one visit I drive the family of Camilo to visit him in a hospital in Granada where he is recovering from an injury.

Sometimes when I drink the good wine from La Mancha in the cave tavern of Ramón de la Toñica, or struggle with the *porrón* in El Miocid with the horse traders of Benalúa, I again compare the Gypsies with another dispersed people, the Jews. They have no Old Testament and they have forgotten that India is their homeland. Yet throughout my travels, I note their pride in being Gypsies and their determination to remain so, despite the pain experienced from holding onto their freedom—something I had learned from Isabel's cry of desperation, "Uglier than a Gypsy!"

Because of it, Antonio, Carlos and all the other *gitanos* are as resistant to assimilation as the twentieth century draws to a close as on their arrival in Iberia at the beginning of the fifteenth, and I feel certain that their descendants will be Gypsies for many years after I voyage to a permanent refuge. It may be that for a few of these years, an occasional Gypsy, whether in Guadix, Badajoz, or Avila will remember the tall *extranjero* who was a friend of the Gypsies while journeying among them, and of whom Rodrigo, the blind lottery vendor, would say, "He is of the family."

# Glossary
## Some Commonly Used Caló Words

| Caló | English | Caló | English |
| --- | --- | --- | --- |
| abiyar | to have | chapires | shoes |
| achantar | to be quiet | chinclí | key |
| anrés | testicles | chinelar | to cut |
| arachí | night | chingar | to fight |
| aratí | blood | chiriclón | chicken |
| bal | hair | chorar | to steal |
| balichón | meat | choro | mule |
| balunes | trousers | chungalo | ugly |
| bandar | to marry | chuquel | dog |
| barím | bride | churí | knife |
| bejañí | guitar | churumbeles | youths |
| ben | devil | coró | pitcher |
| besti | animals | cuchá | breast |
| biñar | to sell | dañí | teeth |
| bocato | hunger | ducais | sorrow |
| brijindar | to rain | errajái | priest |
| bucharnón | bullet | fetel | good |
| bul | anus | gacho | non-Gypsy |
| butal | door | gras | horse |
| cal | penis | gromanje | tomato |
| calé | Gypsy | jalar | to eat |
| cambrí | pregnant | jamar | to eat |
| cangrí | steeple | jel | burro |
| cara | vagina | jillar | vagina |
| chaboró, í | boy, girl | jinar | to defecate |
| chachipé | truth | jojana | lie |
| chanelar | to know | jojoi | rabbit, vagina |

| Caló | English | Caló | English |
| --- | --- | --- | --- |
| jucal | pretty | parne | money |
| junar | to hear; to see | pato, u | father |
| jundunaré | Guardia Civil | payo | non-Gypsy |
| jurdis | powder | peluco | watch |
| lachi | shame | poquinar | to pay |
| lilo | insane | praja | tobacco |
| machón | fish | pus | straw |
| mangar | to beg | quer | house |
| mangué | I; me | querar | to make love |
| manró | bread | ran | staff |
| marar, marelar | to kill | repañé | brandy |
| matipé | drunk | rilar | to break wind; to make love |
| mato, u | mother | | |
| mol | wine | rom, í | man, woman |
| muclar | to urinate | rua | virgin |
| mui | mouth | sacais | eyes |
| mutrar | to urinate | sin | is |
| nahelar | to go | tapiyar | to drink |
| nakí | nose | tatón | bread |
| paluno | farm | trejula | money |
| pañí | water | trupo | body |
| | | undebel | god |
| | | yaquí | fire |

# Suggested Reading


*Exemplary Stories*, Miguel de Cervantes, Penguin Books, New York, 1972.

*The Zincali*, George Borrow, John Murray, London, 1841.

*The Bible in Spain*, George Borrow, John Murray, London, 1843.

*Deep Song*, Irving Brown, Harper, New York, 1929.

*The Gypsy Ballads of García Lorca*, translated by Rolfe Humphries, Indiana University, Bloomington, 1953.

*Don Gypsy*, Walter Starkie, John Murray, London, 1936.

*In Sara's Tents*, Walter Starkie, Dutton, New York, 1953.

*Platero and I*, Juan Ramón Jiménez, New American Library, New York, 1956.

*The Gypsies*, Jean P. Clebert, Penguin, Baltimore, 1967.

*The Gypsies*, Jan Yoors, Simon & Schuster, New York, 1967.

*Gypsies, Wanderers of the World*, Bart McDowell, National Geographic, Washington, D.C., 1970.

*The Art of Flamenco*, Don E. Pohren, Society of Spanish Studies, Seville, 1962.

*Qué Gitano*, Bertha Quintana and Lois Floyd, Holt, Rinehart, New York, 1972.

*Gypsies in the City*, Rena C. Gropper, Darwin Press, Princeton, 1975.

*The Gypsies of Spain*, Jan Yoors, Macmillan, New York, 1974.

# Index

Design by Lynn Springer
Typesetting by Dan Johnson